Lecture Notes in Computer Science 9122

Commenced Publication in 1973
Founding and Former Series Editors:
Gerhard Goos, Juris Hartmanis, and Jan van Leeuwen

More information about this series at http://www.springer.com/series/7411

Steven Latré · Marinos Charalambides
Jérôme François · Corinna Schmitt
Burkhard Stiller (Eds.)

Intelligent Mechanisms for Network Configuration and Security

9th IFIP WG 6.6 International Conference
on Autonomous Infrastructure,
Management, and Security, AIMS 2015
Ghent, Belgium, June 22–25, 2015
Proceedings

 Springer

Editors

Steven Latré
Universiteit Antwerp
Antwerp
Belgium

Corinna Schmitt
Universität Zürich
Zürich
Switzerland

Marinos Charalambides
University College London
London
UK

Burkhard Stiller
Universität Zürich
Zürich
Switzerland

Jérôme François
Inria Nancy Grand Est
Villers-lès-Nancy
France

ISSN 0302-9743   ISSN 1611-3349   (electronic)
Lecture Notes in Computer Science
ISBN 978-3-319-20033-0   ISBN 978-3-319-20034-7   (eBook)
DOI 10.1007/978-3-319-20034-7

Library of Congress Control Number: 2015940762

LNCS Sublibrary: SL5 – Computer Communication Networks and Telecommunications

Springer Cham Heidelberg New York Dordrecht London

Printed on acid-free paper

Springer International Publishing AG Switzerland is part of Springer Science+Business Media
(www.springer.com)

Preface

The International Conference on Autonomous Infrastructure, Management, and Security (AIMS 2015) is a single-track event integrating regular conference paper sessions, tutorials, keynotes, and a PhD student workshop into a highly interactive event. Within the network and service management community, AIMS is focused on PhD students and young researchers. One of the key goals of AIMS is to provide early-stage researchers with constructive feedback by senior scientists and give them the possibility to grow in the research community by means of targeted lab sessions on technical and educational aspects of the research activity. This focus on early-stage researchers is immediately observable in the program, featuring a high number of educational sessions and PhD sessions, where young PhD students present their research.

AIMS 2015 – which took place during June 22–25, 2015, in Ghent, Belgium, and was hosted by Ghent University and iMinds – was the ninth edition of a conference series on management and security aspects of distributed and autonomous systems. It followed the already established tradition of an unusually vivid and interactive conference series, after successful events in Brno, Czech Republic in 2014, Barcelona, Spain in 2013, Luxembourg, Luxembourg in 2012, Nancy, France in 2011, Zürich, Switzerland in 2010, Enschede, The Netherlands in 2009, Bremen, Germany in 2008, and Oslo, Norway in 2007.

This year, AIMS 2015 focused on intelligent mechanisms for network configuration and security. This theme is addressed in the technical program with papers related to monitoring, security, and management methodologies in the application areas of wired and wireless networks, Internet-of-Things, and Cloud infrastructures. AIMS 2015 was organized as a 4-day program to encourage the interaction with and the active participation of the conference's audience. The program consisted of technical sessions for the main track and PhD sessions, interleaved with a research and an educational keynote and three lab sessions.

The lab sessions offered hands-on experience in network and service management topics and they were organized in on-site labs preceded by short tutorial-style teaching sessions. The first tutorial presented the Hadoop framework, explaining common design patterns and how to program using the MapReduce paradigm. The second tutorial covered the topic of deploying Software-Defined Networking (SDN) and Network Functions Virtualization (NFV) on large-scale test-bed facilities. Finally, the third tutorial focused on indexing, searching, and visualizing management tools.

In line with its educational mission, this year the conference also included an educational keynote, which was given by Piet Demeester (Ghent University, iMinds, Belgium) on "Providing Tips and Tricks for Young Researchers" advancing in their PhD career. Additionally, AIMS 2015 featured a research keynote on the "Management of Big Data: The Areas of Conflict" provided by Burkhard Stiller (University of Zürich, Switzerland).

The technical program consisted of two sessions – covering the topics of autonomic and decentralized management, and security, privacy, and management – and included seven full papers, which were selected after a thorough reviewing process out of a total of 22 submissions. Each paper received at least three independent reviews.

The AIMS PhD workshop is a venue for doctoral students to present and discuss their research ideas, and more importantly to obtain valuable feedback from the AIMS audience about their planned PhD research work. This year, the workshop was structured into two technical sessions covering the management of future networks and security management. All PhD papers included in this volume describe the current state of these investigations, including their clear research problem statements, proposed approaches, and an outline of results achieved so far. A total of nine PhD papers were presented and discussed. These papers were selected after a separate review process out of 24 submissions, while all PhD papers received at least three independent reviews, too.

The present volume of the *Lecture Notes in Computer Science* series includes all papers presented at AIMS 2015 as defined within the overall final program. It demonstrates again the European scope of this conference series, since most of the accepted papers originate from European research groups. Also, AIMS 2015 has proven true to its defined DNA of a conference with a strong educational goal, as indicated by the high number of submissions attracted by the PhD Workshop.

The editors would like to thank the many people who helped make AIMS 2015 such a high-quality and successful event. Firstly, many thanks are addressed to all authors, who submitted their contributions to AIMS 2015, and to the lab session speakers, namely, Jérôme François, Niels Bouten, Rachid Mijumbi, Abdelkader Lahmadi, and Frederick Beck, and the keynote speakers Piet Demeester and Burkhard Stiller. The great review work performed by the members of both the AIMS Technical Program Committee and the PhD Student Workshop Committee as well as additional reviewers is highly acknowledged. Thanks are addressed also to Ricardo Schmidt and Tim Wauters for setting up and organizing the lab sessions. Additionally, many thanks are addressed to the local organizers for enabling all logistics and hosting the AIMS 2015 event.

Finally, the editors would like to express their thanks to Springer, and in particular Anna Kramer, for the smooth cooperation in finalizing these proceedings. Additionally, special thanks go to the AIMS 2015 supporters, Ghent University, iMinds, and the European FP7 NoE FLAMINGO under Grant No. 318488.

April 2015   Steven Latré
                                               Marinos Charalambides
                                                      Jérôme François
                                                       Corinna Schmitt

UNIVERSITEIT
GENT

iMinds

NoE FLAMINGO

Organization

General Co-chairs

Filip De Turck   Ghent University, iMinds, Belgium
Piet Demeester   Ghent University, iMinds, Belgium

Technical Program Committee Co-chairs

Steven Latré   University of Antwerp, iMinds, Belgium
Marinos Charalambides   University College London, UK

PhD Student Workshop Co-chairs

Jérôme François   Inria Grand Est Nancy, France
Corinna Schmitt   University of Zürich, Switzerland

Labs Co-chairs

Ricardo Schmidt   University of Twente, The Netherlands
Tim Wauters   Ghent University, iMinds, Belgium

Publications Chair

Burkhard Stiller   University of Zürich, Switzerland

Local Chair

Peter Van Daele   Ghent University, iMinds, Belgium

AIMS Steering Committee

Ramin Sadre   Université Catholique de Louvain, Belgium
Guillaume Doyen   Troyes University of Technology, France
Anna Sperotto   University of Twente, The Netherlands
Pavel Čeleda   Masaryk University, Czech Republic
David Hausheer   Technical University Darmstadt, Germany
Aiko Pras   University of Twente, The Netherlands
Burkhard Stiller   University of Zürich, Switzerland

Technical Program Committee

Alessandro Finamore	Politecnico di Torino, Italy
Alexander Clemm	Cisco Systems, USA
Alexander Keller	IBM Global Technology Services, USA
Alva L. Couch	Tufts University, USA
Anandha Gopalan	Imperial College London, UK
Anna Sperotto	University of Twente, The Netherlands
Bertrand Mathieu	Orange Labs, France
Bruno Quoitin	Université de Mons, Belgium
Daniele Sgandurra	Imperial College London, UK
Danny Raz	Technion, Israel
David Hausheer	Technical University Darmstadt, Germany
Gabi Dreo Rodosek	University of Federal Armed Forces Munich, Germany
Grégory Bonnet	University of Caen Lower Normandy, France
Guillaume Doyen	Troyes University of Technology, France
Isabelle Chrisment	TELECOM Nancy, Université de Lorraine, France
Jan Kořenek	Brno University of Technology, Czech Republic
Jürgen Schönwälder	Jacobs University Bremen, Germany
Kurt Tutschku	Blekinge Institute of Technology, Sweden
Lisandro Zambenedetti Granville	UFRGS, Brazil
Mauro Tortonesi	University of Ferrara, Italy
Michelle Sibilla	Paul Sabatier University, France
Olivier Festor	Telecom Nancy, University of Lorraine, France
Philippe Owezarski	LAAS-CNRS, France
Piotr Cholda	AGH University of Science and Technology, Poland
Ramin Sadre	Université Catholique de Louvain, Belgium
Remi Badonnel	Inria, TELECOM Nancy, Université de Lorraine, France
Thomas Bocek	University of Zürich, Switzerland

PhD Student Workshop Committee

Aiko Pras	University of Twente, The Netherlands
Alberto Schaeffer-Filho	UFRGS, Brazil
Bradley Simmons	Independent Researcher, Canada
Clarissa Marquezan	Huawei European Research Center, Germany
Desislava Dimitrova	University of Bern, Switzerland
Dimitrios Pezaros	University of Glasgow, UK
Jan Vykopal	Masaryk University, Czech Republic
Jeroen Famaey	University of Antwerp, iMinds, Belgium

Joan Serrat	Universitat Politècnica de Catalunya, Spain
Kostas Tsagkaris	University of Piraeus, Greece
Lefteris Mamatas	University College London, UK
Maxwell Young	Drexel University, USA
Paulo Simoes	University of Coimbra, Portugal
Pavel Čeleda	Masaryk University, Czech Republic
Steven Davy	Waterford Institute of Technology, Ireland
Stylianos Georgoulas	University of Surrey, UK
Sven van der Meer	Ericsson, Ireland
Thibault Cholez	Inria Nancy Grand Est, France

Additional Reviewers

Detailed reviews for papers submitted to AIMS 2015 were carried out by the Technical Program Committee as well as the PhD Student Workshop Committee as listed in the previous sections and additionally by the following reviewers:

Alain Ploix
Bart Braem
Christian Koch
Christos Tsiaras
José Jair Santanna
Lautaro Dolberg
Martin Vizváry

Mattijs Jonker
Patrick Truong
Radek Fujdiak
Radhika Garg
Remi Cogranne
Theoni Petropoulou
Vassilis Foteinos

Keynotes

Educational Keynote

Current Trends in Network Research and Advice for Young Researchers

Piet Demeester

Ghent University, iMinds, Belgium
piet.demeester@intec.ugent.be

Abstract. Based on his 30 year of experience in research, this talk will provide a viewpoint on current and important challenges in network-related research. Addressed topics will include wireless networks, Internet-of-Things, Software-defined Networks (SDN), and Network Function Virtualization (NFV): the current status and future perspectives will be addressed. In addition, the importance of Future Internet Research Infrastructures will be stressed and examples will be given of current experimental research facilities.

Furthermore, based on extensive research experience, advice will be provided for young researchers, who want to pursue either an academic career or a career in industry.

Research Keynote

Management of Big Data — The Areas of Conflict: Data Volume, Analysis Methods, and Protection

Burkhard Stiller

Communication Systems Group CSG@IfI
University of Zürich, Zürich, Switzerland
stiller@ifi.uzh.ch

Abstract. In the past decades Information and Communication Technology (ICT) did not only change radically interaction patterns between humans and machines, ICT did more recently enable the support of such enormous Big Data sourcing, especially in terms of volumes transferred, distribution across various distances, and remote correlations of distinct data sets. To an undreamt scale, numbers, facts, and data streams (a) put the challenge onto existing storage architectures, (b) push well-known analysis and data mining methods to and beyond their limits, and (c) result in a major worry to data protection demands. However, without the knowledge of a suitable theory or even a very basic insight into fundamental and coherent relationships of such data, data patterns and data correlations will remain purely random.

Thus, this keynote will introduce and partially define the term "Big Data", it will discuss the embedding of Big Data into today's society, and will work out key details of the Big Data management dimension, driven by selected examples, which face a diversity of opportunities and risks.

Due to the fact that traditional and technical constraints of ICT are today oversteered by emerging economic and security-related perspectives, large data sets — by now commonly termed as Big Data — outline a broad set of challenges in terms of (a) the identity protection of the individual or selected single data items, (b) the statistical validity of analysis methods, and (c) the raise and effect of initially unknown or unintended meta data becoming part of a new analysis. All approaches technically doable today may be ethically questionable, although legally justifiable, since suitable privacy laws are not in place yet. Finally, by taking a look into the future, a picture is crafted carefully consisting of current trends and visions, which offer opportunities for the development of new big data management mechanisms.

Lab Sessions

Lab Session 1

Map-Reduce and Hadoop

Jérôme François

Inria Grand Est Nancy, France
`jerome.francois@inria.fr`

Abstract. This tutorial introduces Hadoop and how it can be applied to different challenges today's community is facing in network management. Data analytics is, thus, the focus of this tutorial as networks are producing tons of various logs, for example network traffic measures, firewall alerts, or SNMP messages. They form the basis of many management functions, which may necessitate basic processing like accounting or more complex calculations in particular for providing predictions on the future for (a) configuration purposes, (b) detecting security anomalies, or (c) supporting fault management.

This lab session introduces the Map-Reduce paradigm before explaining how to implement a program for Hadoop. Common programming patterns (join, filter, aggregation) are presented using short examples. Usual problems are discussed also, for example sorting or optimizing and chaining multiple tasks. Finally, the lab session presents Hadoop extensions like Pig for writing requests without any programming needs.

Lab Session 2

Deploying Network Function Virtualization Experiments on the Virtual Wall Test-Bed

Niels Bouten[1] and Rashid Mijumbi[2]

[1] Ghent University, iMinds, Belgium
[2] Universitat Politècnica de Catalunya, Spain
niels.bouten@intec.ugent.be, rashid@tsc.upc.edu

Abstract. Network Function Virtualization (NFV) takes advantage of IT virtualization technologies and network programming to virtualize physical network functions (e.g., firewall, NAT, and DHCP) and interconnect them to create new communication services. This allows service providers to create new communication services on top of existing network and datacenter infrastructure enabling shorter time-to-market at lower cost. Combining IT virtualization and Software-defined Networking (SDN) technologies allows NFV to increase greatly the network management flexibility by decoupling network functions from physical machines and by decoupling the control plane from traffic forwarding in network equipment.

The goal of this hands-on tutorial is to familiarize all participants with the concept of NFV in general and possible benefits of combining it with SDN. This will be accomplished by deploying several network functions on the Virtual Wall and interconnecting them using OpenFlow. This allows for the creation of individual Service Function Chains (SFC) for different users.

These experiments will be run in a live network setting, facilitated by the Virtual Wall test-bed. The Virtual Wall is a test-bed facility for setting up large-scale network topologies. Its nodes can be assigned different functionality and organized in arbitrary network topologies on the fly. As such, it is a generic experimental environment for advanced network, distributed software and service evaluation, and supports scalability research. The facility has been made available to the research community through different FP7 FIRE projects. This tutorial will provide, too, a brief theoretical introduction about the Virtual Wall's capabilities in preparation of the hands-on part. By using the jFed framework for test-bed federation, experiments on the Virtual Wall will be set-up.

Lab Session 3

Powering Monitoring Analytics with ELK Stack

Abdelkader Lahmadi[1] and Frederick Beck[2]

[1] University of Lorraine, France
[2] INRIA Nancy, France
abdelkader.lahmadi@loria.fr, frederic.beck@inria.fr

Abstract. Machine-generated data, including logs and network flows, are considerably growing and their collection, searching, and visualization is a challenging task for (a) daily administrator activities and (b) researchers aiming to better find out analytics and insights from monitoring data regarding their research goals, including amongst others security or modeling of network and systems.

This lab session introduces the open source ELK stack and its components, including Elasticsearch for deep search and data analytics, Logstash for centralized logging, log enrichment, and parsing, and Kibana for powerful and beautiful data visualizations. ELK enables the analysis and visualization of monitoring data, such as logs and netflows. A first step details these individual components and the second step provides guidelines for their deployment and configuration. In the third step participants will perform hands-on practical work for collecting, processing, and enriching logs and netflows, combined with the creation of associated visualization and dashboards aspects.

Contents

Ph.D. Student Workshop — Security Management

Autonomic and Decentralized Management

Disruption-Free Link Wake-Up Optimisation
for Energy Aware Networks

Obinna Okonor[✉], Ning Wang, Zhili Sun, and Stylianos Georgoulas

Institute for Communication Systems, University of Surrey, Guildford, Surrey,
GU2 7XH, UK
{o.okonor,n.wang,z.sun,s.georgoulas}@surrey.ac.uk

Abstract. Energy efficiency has become a major research topic in the Internet community as a result of unprecedented rise in the Information and Communication Technology (ICT) sector. One typical approach towards energy efficiency is to select a subset of IP routers or interfaces that will go to sleep mode during the off-peak period. However, on-the-fly network reconfiguration is generally deemed harmful especially to real time packets due to routing reconvergence. In this paper, we develop an efficient algorithm for achieving energy efficiency which is disruption free. The objective is to incrementally wake up sleeping links upon the detection of increased traffic demand. Unlike normal approaches of manipulating link weights or reverting to full topology in case of even minor network congestion and thereby sacrificing energy savings, our algorithm wakes up the minimum number of sleeping links to the network in order to handle this dynamicity. The performance of our algorithm was evaluated using the GEANT network topology and its traffic traces over a period of one week. According to our simulation results, up to almost 47% energy gains can be achieved without any obstruction to the network performance. Secondly, we show that the activation of a small number of sleeping links is still sufficient to cope with the observed traffic surge.

1 Introduction

The recent rapid growth of Internet has led to the unprecedented rise in energy consumption. According to a number of studies, ICT alone contributes up to 2 – 10% of world's power consumption and this is expected to rise in the near future [1 – 5]. The issue is that there is high level of bandwidth resource underutilisation in the current Internet due to over-provisioning of resources by telecom operators. However, this figure does not depict the actual power usage since the power consumption of networking devices does not scale with current load. On the other hand, with the advent of real time streaming multimedia applications which often require reliable network connectivity, the re-convergence period of the IP routing tables upon topology changes poses a major concern if sleeping and restoration technologies are applied. Typically, current interior gateway protocols (IGPs) like Open Shortest Path First (OSPF) or Intermediate System - Intermediate System (IS-IS) take about hundreds of milliseconds to re-converge, which is not desired when supporting seamless

© IFIP International Federation for Information Processing 2015
S. Latré et al. (Eds.): AIMS 2015, LNCS 9122, pp. 3–16, 2015.
DOI: 10.1007/978-3-319-20034-7_1

transmission of real-time multimedia content. The use of IP Fast ReRoute (IPFRR) has been proposed by Internet Engineering Task force (IETF) to reduce the reaction time to tens of milliseconds [6, 7].

A common practice for achieving energy efficiency following a time driven approach is to pre-configure a network topology with reduced capacity for energy savings during a given period of off-peak time. This is because network devices consume maximum amount of energy on both idle and underutilised conditions [29]. However, the assumption is that within this energy saving period, the network will be able to handle any traffic surge without causing traffic congestion. This implies that the only solution to tackle unexpected traffic surge beyond the reduced network capacity is to revert to the full network topology and thereby sacrificing energy savings. In most cases, one may observe that the *incremental* wake-up of a small number of sleeping links back to the working state could have handled such traffic uncertainty. In addition, in order to avoid traffic disruptions caused by routing re-convergence upon link wake-up operations, it is also desirable to prioritise the wake-up of those links which will not incur any routing re-convergence and, as a consequence, traffic disruption.

In this work, we propose an efficient algorithm for incremental and opportunistic link wake up operation when it is necessary. We exploit the fact that since many links are underutilised when traffic demand is low during off-peak time, putting such links to sleep mode without incurring traffic congestion to the remaining active links leads to significant energy savings. Based on the reduced topology, we propose an algorithm called Disruption-free Link Wake-up Optimisation Technique (DLiWOT) for enabling incremental link wake-up operations. Upon the detection of network congestion at some active links, this algorithm aims to identify the minimum set of sleeping links to wake up in order to handle potential congestion, while still leaving the remaining sleeping links in standby mode for energy efficiency. The novelty here is a disruption-free proactive mechanism to incrementally avoid congestion risks without necessarily resorting to full topology activation.

According to OSPF/ISIS operation, upon a topology change (e.g. when a link is added to the active network topology), all affected routers need to update their respective routing tables upon re-calculating shortest paths to their destinations. This transient period of several hundred milliseconds poses potential disruption to real time traffic flows. By taking into account this issue, we design the DLiWOT scheme for waking up sleeping links but without incurring any re-convergence procedure. Specifically, the wake up of such links remains only known by their head nodes which will then intelligently divert traffic onto them *locally*, but without further announcing these newly added links to any other remote routers. This is the main improvement with respect to our previous work in [8]. In order to realise DLiWOT, we employed the same network monitoring and control technique as in [9]. In this approach, with the help of traffic engineering (TE) link state advertisements (LSAs) [10], a network control server (NCS) keeps a logical view of the network topology and traffic conditions. The NCS periodically monitors the network conditions at a given time interval which can be determined by the network administrator. Upon the detection of any active link suffering from congestion, the NCS then applies DLiWOT to identify the necessary sleeping links to wake up for traffic diversion. It is also the responsibility of the NCS to actually trigger the wake-up of the identified sleeping links for appropriate traffic diversion.

As we will show through simulations using the GEANT network topology and its real historical traffic traces, DLiWOT is capable of achieving significant energy gains of up to almost 47%, compared to using the full network topology for congestion alleviation, and in a completely disruption-free manner at all times.

2 Related Work

This section summarises relevant works for achieving green ISP networks. Since the amount of energy saving depends on the number of removed links, most existing energy schemes rely on link removal as the main energy saving strategy. Research has also shown that line cards contribute up to 43% of routers energy consumption [11, 12], so link (and the associated line card) sleeping, when implemented properly, can lead to significant overall energy savings. The authors of [13] first suggested a number of approaches for energy savings in the current Internet. These include both network-wide and link-level approaches. According to the network-wide approach, during low link utilisation, the traffic is aggregated into few routes in order to turn off some router interfaces to sleep mode. Link-level approaches involve only local decisions without affecting the operation of the entire network. Numerous proposals have been made in the literature which are summarised in [14, 15].

It has been observed that many operational networks have diurnal traffic patterns that can be regular [16] and this is exploited in energy savings as in [17]. The authors propose a time-driven link sleeping algorithm for energy savings that deploys a multi topology routing protocol to switch between full and reduced topology. In [18], the number of network configurations was considered. The authors showed that their algorithm is able to identify the minimum number of network configurations and time duration within a day for them to be enforced. This maximises energy savings and minimises protocol overhead. However, this is on the condition that regular traffic matrices (TMs) are applied which is not always the case and therefore does not guarantee network robustness to dynamic traffic conditions.

Concerning the issue of routing re-convergence, the authors of [19] propose a hybrid IP-MPLS solution during transient periods for re-convergence avoidance. The authors of [20] propose an offline algorithm for selecting links whose set of traffics can be rerouted in the network without causing any traffic disruption and using the existing Fast Reroute technique, the traffic can be diverted. The authors of [21] investigate the manipulation of network link weights in order to redirect traffic to a particular path while the free links are set to sleep mode for energy savings. Also, [22] employs the use of link weight manipulation in such a way that each step is loop free. A resource management approach was employed in [28] while [29] considered hardware support for online traffic scaling. In [8], the wake up scheme does not consider the routing convergence of the whole network; [23] deployed a combined layer approach by using dynamic circuit to establish bypass links. However, our work is purely a non-disruptive IP layer approach with no additional cost at the routing protocol level.

3   Problem Statement

Let us consider a directed and connected network graph G consisting of a set of vertices V, connected by a set of edges E, and denoted as G (V, E). V represents the network nodes/routers while E represents the set of network links. $N = |V|$ is the total number of nodes and $L = |E|$ is the total number of links in the network. Each link is associated with a link weight for computing shortest paths in IP routing and all links are assumed to be symmetrical. Table 1 below summarises specific parameters associated with the problem.

Table 1. List of Symbols

Variable	Description
P_{ef}	Energy efficiency
ℓ_{ij}	Link connecting nodes i & j in that direction
t^{sd}	Total traffic demand from source (s) to destination (d)
ℓ_{ij}^{sd}	Traffic flow from s - d that is routed through ℓ_{ij}
L_{ij}	Total traffic load on link ℓ_{ij}
T	Threshold value for network link utilisation conditions
c_{ij}	Link Bandwidth
S_c^{sd}	Set of links in congested path routing traffic from s to d
S_n^{sd}	Set of links in new path routing traffic from s to d
ℓ_c	Congested link
E_s	Set of sleeping links

We therefore formulate an Integer Liner Programming (ILP) formulation of our problem where the objective function is to maximise P_{ef} subject to the constraints as explained below:

$$max\ P_{ef} \tag{1}$$

Subject to:

$$\sum_{j=1}^{N} \ell_{ij}^{sd} - \sum_{j=1}^{N} \ell_{ji}^{sd} = \begin{cases} t^{sd}, & \forall s, d, i = s \\ -t^{sd}, & \forall s, d, i = d \\ 0, & \forall s, d, i \neq s, d \end{cases} \tag{2}$$

$$\frac{1}{c_{ij}} L_{ij} \leq T \quad \forall \{i, j\} \in E \tag{3}$$

$$S_n^{sd} \cap \ell_c = \emptyset \qquad \forall s, d \,|\, \ell_c \notin E_s \tag{4}$$

The objective function of our research work is to increase network energy saving gains as much as possible, which is stated in equation (1). Equation (2) is the flow conservation constraint such that $\ell_{ij}^{sd} \geq 0$ over any network link where s and d are such that $\{s, d\} \in V$. Equation (3) preserves the individual link utilisation and by extension, the maximum link utilisation (MLU) in the network. This implies that it controls the congestion level of the network. Once the value of MLU is more than the set threshold, the network is considered to be congested. Note also that this equation is the primary determinant for the number of links that can go to sleep or need to be woken up in the network. The higher the threshold value, the more the chances of links to be put to sleep and fewer links to be woken up to handle traffic upsurge. Also, the considered TM contributes to the number of initially pruned links in the network; as such, deploying the TM with the least utilisation level for the period of consideration gives maximum link removal. The selection of the minimum number of links to wake up in order to alleviate congestion as a result of traffic surge is stated in equation (4) and should be such that if –

$$S_c^{sd} = \{s, R_1, R_2, R_3, \dots, d\} \tag{5}$$

where R_1, R_2, R_3 are the set of nodes of the congested path and the congested link is, for example, $\ell_c = \ell(R_1 \rightarrow R_2)$, then, S_n^{sd} must not contain $\ell(R_1 \rightarrow R_2)$ such that equation (4) is obeyed. This constraint makes it possible that at each iteration of the algorithm, only the shortest path that excludes the congested link will be considered during wake up operation.

The value of P_{ef} can be evaluated by considering the energy consumed by the full and pruned topology respectively. More so, since some links are woken up to the network within some time interval during operational runtime, the link power contributions are also considered as shown in equation (6). P_f and P_p represent the energy consumption of the full and pruned topologies respectively while P_w is the energy consumption of the wake up links.

$$P_{ef} = \frac{\sum P_f - \sum P_p + \sum P_w}{\sum P_f} \tag{6}$$

The presented ILP falls under the class of capacitated multi-commodity minimum cost flow problem and is known to be NP-hard [24]. Therefore, only trivial cases like small networks can be solved using exact method. As such, we explore a heuristic approach to solving it.

4 Scheme Description

Before presenting the generic algorithm, we first illustrate the core underlying principle using the synthetic network topology in Fig. 1.

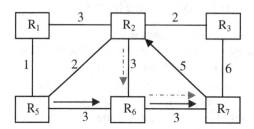

Fig. 1. A synthetic network topology

The network contains 6 nodes and 18 symmetrical links of equal bandwidth capacity of 10 Mbps. Let's assume that $\ell(R_2 \to R_7)$ is the only sleeping link with the assigned link weight of 5 (as such, the directed arrow in Fig. 1 means that between R_2 and R_7, only $\ell(R_7 \to R_2)$ is active). Assume that at time t_1, the following source destination pairs route 5 Mbps of traffic in the network: $\{R_5, R_7\}$ through $R_5 \to R_6 \to R_7$, and $\{R_2, R_7\}$ through $R_2 \to R_6 \to R_7$. This implies that the link load on $\ell(R_6 \to R_7)$ at that time becomes 10 Mbps, implying a link utilisation of 100%. Assume a link utilisation threshold of 90% indicates that a link is vulnerable to congestion. In this case, if $\ell(R_2 \to R_7)$ is added to the network in order to relieve congestion by diverting traffic away from link $l(R_6 \to R_7)$, routing of R_5 does not change since R_5 does not make use of $\ell(R_2 \to R_7)$ to route traffic (whether active or non active). Only traffic from R_2 is diverted through $\ell(R_2 \to R_7)$. We refer to such links as stub links – a stub link   is a link that is used by only its own head node for traffic forwarding, but no traffic originated further beyond the local head is routed through this link. It can be inferred that existence of stub links depend on the physical network topology as well as its IGP link weight setting. As such, when restored to the topology for congestion avoidance, even if their restoration is advertised to remote routers, it does not lead to any remote router updating its routing table. If we now consider that the link $\ell(R_2 \to R_7)$ has a link weight of 3 instead of 5 as used before, the routing of the network will change during the wake up process. In that case, if the link is restored to alleviate congestion and its restoration is advertised to the remote routers, router R_5, in addition to router R_2, will also use the advertised link to route traffic to R_7. This can be referred to as congestion diversion instead of congestion avoidance since the utilisation of the added link $\ell(R_2 \to R_7)$ will become the same as that of the previous congested link in the network i.e. $\ell(R_6 \to R_7)$. In that case, link $\ell(R_2 \to R_7)$ can be said to be a transit link - transit links are those links that can be used by other remote nodes to route traffics and therefore are prone to causing disruption when added to the network [8]. It is also worth noting that the classification of these links is based on the pruned topology.

Detailed Operation of DLiWOT - due to the dynamicity of today's traffic, the wake-up algorithm is provided as a proactive measure to control network traffic. DLiWOT is an online congestion control algorithm that is executed at the NCS which exploits the traffic engineering opportunity provided by IP interior routing protocols like OSPF and traffic measurements. This is unlike most energy saving schemes that combine the functionalities of both IP and other existing networks. De facto, OSPF-TE provides special technique for optimising operational performance of a network through the use of opaque LSAs in disseminating TE information. Such TE-LSAs contain basic information for the NCS's decision which includes: maximum link bandwidth, TE metric, router address type/length/value etc. This is in contrast with the normal paradigm in traditional OSPF which is based on static path routing without recourse to network utilisations or energy efficiency, except link bandwidth.

The NCS periodically polls this information from each node, and hence, is able to keep a record of the details of the traffic conditions within the network. The link utilisation is calculated at a certain period of time according to the network administrator's preference. Once it exceeds a set threshold value, DLiWOT is applied by the NCS to identify the alternative paths for possible diversion of traffic from the congested links (see Fig. 2 for the DLiWOT algorithm). This is done by identifying the source nodes of the traffic flows through the congested links and sorting them in a descending order according to their respective bandwidth demands. The descending order approach helps in preventing waking up of excessive sleeping links since only the minimum number of flows (causing the link to be above the utilisation threshold) will need to be diverted instead of many low demand flows possibly scattered along different routes. The selection of the minimum number of links to wake up in order to support any traffic surge should be such that equation (4) is adhered to. Therefore, the set of links on the new path should be devoid of the congested link if traffic is to be diverted away from it, while still maintaining the source-destination pairs of the packet. Secondly, the network threshold value must conform to equation (3). That is, no link's utilisation should be higher than the set threshold value at any point in time; otherwise, the link is said to be congested. The variables x, y, and m are used in the algorithm as counters. In order to adhere to the re-convergence avoidance criteria, selection of stub links is prioritised. This is because the addition of stub link does not cause the diversion of any traffic originated from remote nodes, except the local traffic originated by the head node of the added link. As such, for stub link wake up, there does not need to be any special action taken to prevent link advertisements from reaching remote routers. Each packet flow in the network consists of packet source and destination in its packet header. Therefore, DLiWOT initially checks if each flow's source node has any sleeping stub link that can possibly divert such traffic away from the congested link as shown in the algorithm. If such link exists, the link is added into the logical topology and the MLU of the network is recalculated to ensure that the added link does not cause congestion to the alternate path. If the network is free from congestion, the algorithm returns the current topology to the active state; otherwise, the next stub link is explored. This process is continued for transit sleeping links only if the addition of stub links does not resolve the network congestion. In transit link consideration, in order not to cause traffic disruption, transit link restoration is not advertised, so remote routers remain oblivious to the changes in the topology due to the restored link(s). The NCS locally activates the transit links in order to alleviate the congestion at that period of time.

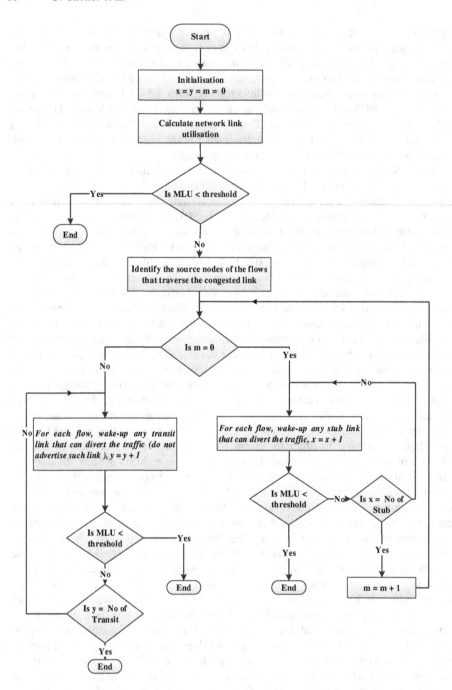

Fig. 2. Proposed DLiWOT algorithm for link wake-up

5   Performance Evaluation

It can be easily inferred that the proposed link wake up technique can be applied on top of any existing link sleeping optimisation scheme which provides the input of the pruned topology. There can be two common options of deploying the pruned topology, and using DLiWOT to restore sleeping links to it: (1) applying the pruned topology at the lowest utilisation point within every 24 hour period and use DLiWOT till the end of the pre-defined off-peak period; and (2) applying the pruned topology at the beginning of the off-peak period and use DLiWOT till its end. In this paper, we chose the second option. In our case, off peak period is defined from 8 PM to 8 AM, meaning that the pruned topology is applied at 8 PM every day and DLiWOT is applied from 8PM until 8 AM. During the peak period, the full topology is used. The determination of the off-peak time is up to the operator, and in this paper the chosen period is only representative.

In order to assess the performance of our algorithm, we consider the GEANT operational network in which the TMs vary according to a "peak- off-peak" pattern. The GEANT topology is an operational network in Europe for research purposes with 23 point-of-presence nodes, and 74 links. The TMs used for the simulation contain 672 traffic matrix instances generated in one week at every 15 minutes interval [25]. Furthermore, we took into account that the actual energy consumption of a link is not proportional to the link utilisation rate but on the power consumption of the line cards [26]. Therefore, we deployed the energy consumption model of the line cards as stated in Table 2 in calculating their respective energy rates and the savings.

Table 2. Power consumption rate of router's line cards [11, 27]

Line card	Speed (bps)	Power (Watts)
1-Port OC-192	9953280	174
2-Port OC-48	4976640	160
1-Port OC-48	2488320	140
1-Port OC-3	155520	60

Fig. 3 compares the average utilisation level of the original full topology with topology derived using the DLiWOT scheme using the pruned topology as a starting point. As it can be seen, during the period under consideration, there is an increase in the average link utilisation (ALU) for DLiWOT in all the seven days. This means that the application of DLiWOT can minimise underutilisation while providing energy savings at the same time. The lower spikes correspond to weekend traffic, when traffic is at its lowest value. For example, in the first day during the off peak period when the algorithm was deployed, the highest ALU of the full topology is barely 6% while it is more than double when DLiWOT was applied.

Another novelty of our algorithm is that the congestion control is network based and not link based. This implies that if there is congestion at more than one link, the algorithm returns the minimum number of links to relieve all congestions and in a non disruptive way. Fig. 4 shows the performance of the algorithm when applied to GEANT for a period of 7 days based on the MLU. The graph shows that despite the application of a pruned topology over the considered period, the MLU is not more than 100%. This is based on the deployment of DLiWOT. For example, during our simulations, the number of added sleeping links during the week is shown in Fig. 5. The TM id depicts the actual traffic matrix that caused the congestion while the vertical axis depicts the number of woken up links to control such congestion. In the graph, it is obvious that just the addition of 4 links in each case controlled such congestion while other schemes would have reverted to the full topology and thereby waking more than 30 links up. The number of added links also affected the energy savings in the period as shown in Table 3. Therefore, one can infer that the addition of few links can actually keep the congestion level below a set threshold instead of reverting to the full topology and thereby sacrificing energy savings. Due to the robustness of our scheme in congestion control, its application period can be extended for use beyond the off-peak period. The only difference being that more links may have to wake up during the peak period, if congestion occurs.

As mentioned, in order to control traffic disruption during wake up of links and minimise the number of link restoration advertisements that need to be prevented from reaching remote routers, DLiWOT prioritises the waking up of stub links before transit links. For transit links addition, the links are not advertised to the network. Therefore, the added links do not result to any count to infinity or bouncing effect.

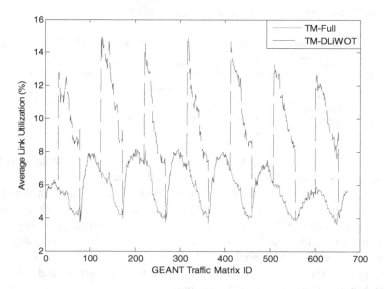

Fig. 3. ALU performance based on "full" and "pruned topology with DLiWOT" during off peak period over 7 days

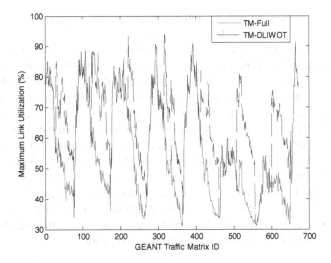

Fig. 4. MLU performance based on "full" and "pruned topology with DLiWOT" during off peak period over 7 days

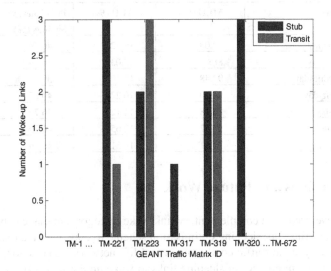

Fig. 5. Performance of DLiWOT in terms of waking up of links within a week interval

Table 3 describes the different attributes of the pruned topology with regards to performance metrics. It shows that the reduced topology of GEANT, when applied and used subsequently by DLiWOT, leads to an ALU of about 2.5 times than that of the full topology (see also Fig. 3). This is an indication of more balanced use of network resources in our case and significant reduction in network resource underutilisation. ALU is also dependent on the threshold settings, which in our simulations was set to 95% in order to be proactive to congestion. Therefore, our algorithm is developed in such a way that it controls traffics on the network based on threshold settings, which can be tuned by a network operator depending on their preferences about pro-activity to congestion and acceptable MLU levels.

On the energy savings, Table 3 shows a substantial amount of savings on a daily basis (only during off-peak periods) which is dependent on the number of sleeping links and also on their power consumption characteristics (note that the links have different power consumption characteristics; as such the energy savings are directly proportional to the power of individual links as shown in Table 2). As shown, the MLU within this period does not exceed the threshold value (see Fig. 4) despite the reduced number of active links. In this case, once the network MLU reaches the threshold value, DLiWOT is immediately deployed to control such congestion and reduce MLU below the pre-defined 95% threshold. It is also important to note that during the weekends, the off peak period can be extended because of the very low traffic, meaning that an operator can apply the DLiWOT scheme for longer time periods (which can be considered as off-peak well beyond the considered here 8PM-8AM period), thereby extending even more the energy saving gains.

Table 3. Performance analysis of TM attributes for one week during the off peak period when DLiWOT is applied

Days	MLU (%)	ALU (%)	Pef - Energy Savings (%)
Monday	85.08	10.42	46.79
Tuesday	88.81	12.03	46.79
Wednesday	93.48	10.10	39.82
Thursday	94.00	10.22	40.87
Friday	82.18	11.12	46.79
Saturday	80.87	10.65	46.79
Sunday	75.51	10.31	46.79

6 Conclusions and Future Work

In this paper, we propose a complementary link wake up algorithm that can be applied on top of any existing link sleeping optimisation scheme to cope with the existence of uncertainty and dynamic traffic conditions in real life networks. The algorithm aims to select the minimum number of sleeping links to wake up during traffic surge without causing any form of traffic disruption. This is in contrast to most works that unnecessarily sacrifice energy savings once there is traffic surge in the network or provide backup paths in the pruned topology as a proactive measure to congestion avoidance. To this end, we also answer a key research question on how to handle traffic surge without disruption. We demonstrate through our simulations that our scheme can be able to save substantial amounts of energy and is also robust to traffic dynamicity in a disruption free manner. More so, our scheme does not depend on the combination of different network platform for its operation i.e. operates purely in an IP based platform alone. The obtained results showed significant energy savings and improved link utilisation without sacrificing network efficiency. It is a novel approach to today's network for possible adoption by ISPs whose paramount desire is to save energy without traffic disruption. This has also shown that adopting link sleeping mode is a realistic approach with no modification to the traditional IP forwarding protocols required.

In future work, we intend to investigate how we can explore putting back some links to sleeping mode after wake up so that the scheme can be applied seamlessly throughout the whole operational runtime of a network, maximising even further the opportunities for energy savings by "tracking" both increases and also decreases in network traffic demand conditions.

Acknowledgement. This research was funded by the EPSRC Knowledge-Centric Networking (KCN) project (EP/L026120/1).

References

1. Vereecken, W., Deboosere, L., Colle, D., Vermeulen, B., Pickavet, M.: Energy Efficiency in Telecommunication Networks. In: European Conference on Networks and Optical Communications (NOC), Krems, Austria, July 01-03, pp. 44–51 (2008)
2. Server and Data Center Energy Efficiency, Final Report to Congress, U.S. Environmental Protection Agency (2007)
3. Hlavacs, H., Costa, G., Pierson, J.: Energy Consumption of Residential and Professional Switches. In: Proceedings of the IEEE International Conference on Computational Science and Engineering, pp. 240–246 (August 2009)
4. Vereecken, W., Deboosere, L., Colle, D., Vermeulen, B., Pickavet, M., Dhoedt, B., Demeester, P.: Energy efficiency in telecommunication networks. In: Proc. NOC, Krems, Austria, pp. 44–51 (July 2008)
5. Baliga, J., Hinton, K., Tucker, R.S.: Energy Consumption of the Internet. In: Joint International Conference on Optical Internet, 2007 and the 32nd Australian Conference on Optical Fibre Technology (COIN-ACOFT 2007), pp. 1–3 (June 2007)
6. Retvari, G., Tapolcai, J., Enyedi, G., Csaszar, A.: IP Fast ReRoute: Loop Free Alternative Revisted. In: INFOCOM, pp. 2948–2956 (2011)
7. Shand, M., Bryant, S.: IP Fast Reroute framework. RFC 5714 (January 2010)
8. Okonor, O., Wang, N., Sun, Z., Georgoulas, S.: Link Sleeping and Wake-up Optimization for Energy Aware ISP Networks. IEEE-ISCC (2014)
9. Wang, N., Ho, K.-H., Pavlou, G.: Adaptive multi-topology IGP based traffic engineering with near-optimal network performance. In: Das, A., Pung, H.K., Lee, F.B.S., Wong, L.W.C. (eds.) NETWORKING 2008. LNCS, vol. 4982, pp. 654–666. Springer, Heidelberg (2008)
10. Katz, D., Kompella, K., Yeung, D.: (September 2003), http://tools.ietf.org/html/rfc3630
11. Li, Q., Xu, M., Yang, Y., Gao, L., et al.: Safe and Practical Energy-Efficient Detour Routing in IP Networks. IEEE/ACM Transactions on Networking (99), 1925–1937 (2013)
12. Baliga, J., Ayre, R., Hinton, K., Tucher, R.: Energy Consumption in Wired Access Networks. IEEE Communication Magazines 49(6) (June 2011)
13. Gupta, M., Singh, S.: Greening of the Internet. In: ACM SIGCOMM, Karlsruhe, Germany (August 2003)

14. Bianzino, A.P., Chaudet, C., Rossi, D., Rougier, J.: A survey of green networking research. IEEE Communications Surveys & Tutorials 14(1), 3–20 (2012)
15. Bolla, R., Bruschi, R., Davoli, F., Cucchietti, F.: Energy Efficiency in the Future Internet: A Survey of Existing Approaches and Trends in Energy-Aware Fixed Network Infrastructures. IEEE Communications Surveys & Tutorials 13(2) (July 2010)
16. Roughan, M., Greenberg, A., Kalmanek, C., Rumsewicz, M., Yates, J., Zhang, Y.: Experience in measuring backbone traffic variability: models, metrics, measurements and meaning. In: Proceedings of the 2nd ACM SIGCOMM Workshop on Internet Measurement, IMW 2002, New York, NY, USA, pp. 91–92 (2002)
17. Francois, F., Wang, N., Moessner, K., Georgoulas, S.: Optimization for Time-driven Link Sleeping Reconfigurations in ISP Backbone Networks. In: Network Operations and Management Symposium (NOMS). IEEE (April 2012)
18. Chiaraviglio, L., Cianfrani, A.: On the Effectiveness of Sleep Modes in Backbone Networks with Limited Configurations. In: Software, Telecommunications and Computer Networks (SoftCOM), Italy (2012)
19. Skivee, F., Balon, S., Leduc, G.: A Scalable heuristic for hubrid IGP/MPLS traffic engineering - Case study on an operational network. In: IEEE International Conference on Networks, Singapore, (2006)
20. Wang, N., Michael, C., Ho, K.H.: "Disruption-free green traffic engineering with NotVia fast reroute. IEEE Communications Letters 15(10), 1123–1125 (2011)
21. Gao, S., Zhou, J., Yamanaka, N.: Reducing Network Consumption Using Dynamic Link Metric Method and Power Off Links. In: 1st Telecom PARISTECH-KEIO University Workshop Future Networking, France (September 2010)
22. Francois, P., Shand, M., Bonaventure, O.: Disruption Free Topology Reconfiguration in OSPF Networks. In: 26th IEEE International Conference on Computer Communications, IEEE INFOCOM (2007)
23. Chamania, M., Caria, M., Jukan, A.: Effective Usage of Dynamic Circuits for IP Routing. IEEE ICC (2010)
24. Chiaraviglio, L., Mellia, M., Neri, F.: Reducing Power Consumption in Backbone Networks. In: IEEE International Conference on Communications, Germany ICC (2009)
25. The GEANT Network, http://www.geant.net
26. Chabarek, J., Sommers, J., et al.: Power awareness in network design and routing. In: INFOCOM (2008)
27. Cisco 12000 series Packet Over SONET/SDH (POS) line cards, http://www.cisco.com/en/US/prod/collateral/routers/ps6342/product_data_sheet0900aecd803fd7b9.pdf
28. Charalambides, M., Tuncer, D., Mamatas, L., Pavlou, G.: Energy - Aware Adaptive Network Resource Management. In: Proc. 2013 of the IFIP/IEEE Integrated Management Symposium (May 2013)
29. Vasić, N., Kostić, D.: Energy-aware traffic engineering. In: Proceedings of the 1st International Conference on Energy-Efficient Computing and Networking. ACM (2010)

Towards the Description and Execution of Transitions in Networked Systems

Alexander Frömmgen[1](✉), Björn Richerzhagen[2], Julius Rückert[3],
David Hausheer[3], Ralf Steinmetz[2], and Alejandro Buchmann[1]

[1] Databases and Distributed Systems, TU Darmstadt, Darmstadt, Germany
{froemmge,buchmann}@dvs.tu-darmstadt.de
[2] Multimedia Communications Lab, TU Darmstadt, Darmstadt, Germany
{bjoern.richerzhagen,ralf.steinmetz}@kom.tu-darmstadt.de
[3] Peer-to-Peer Systems Engineering Lab, TU Darmstadt, Darmstadt, Germany
{rueckert,hausheer}@ps.tu-darmstadt.de

Abstract. Today's distributed systems have to work in changing environments and under different working conditions. To provide high performance under these changing conditions, many distributed systems implement adaptive behavior. While simple adaptation through parameter tuning can only react to a limited range of conditions, a switch between different mechanisms at runtime enables broader adaptivity. However, distributed systems that switch mechanisms at runtime lack a clear abstraction for the adaptive behavior and, thus, usually interleave the adaptation and actual application logic. This leads to complex and error-prone systems that are hard to maintain and not easy to extend.

In this paper, we analyze the adaptations of two distributed systems from different application domains. We identify recurring requirements as well as life cycles of transitions between mechanisms. Based on this, we present a framework that provides a clear abstraction of the underlying transition logic and manages the transitions at runtime. The concept is applied to the two example systems to practically evaluate its benefits. We show that our approach leads to less complex realizations of the adaptive behavior and allows new mechanisms to be integrated easily.

1 Introduction

Today's distributed systems operate in challenging environments with rapidly changing working conditions. In order to provide high performance in such dynamic environments, systems need to be highly adaptive. However, simple adaptations by means of configuration parameter adjustments can only react to a limited range of conditions. As distributed systems can be described as a combination of multiple functional blocks, in the following called *Mechanisms*, the ability to switch between mechanisms at runtime and the possibility to extend the system by novel mechanism, proved to provide greater flexibility and enables the system to adapt to a wider range of environmental conditions [14,18]. In the following, such switches between mechanisms are referred to as *Transitions*.

© IFIP International Federation for Information Processing 2015
S. Latré et al. (Eds.): AIMS 2015, LNCS 9122, pp. 17–29, 2015.
DOI: 10.1007/978-3-319-20034-7_2

While this idea is appealing, so far, there exists neither a systematic approach of how to generically integrate multiple mechanisms in a complex distributed system, nor how to systematically execute and coordinate transitions between mechanisms at runtime. The latter is especially challenging as it requires a deep understanding of mechanism life cycles and a generic approach for state transfers between mechanisms in transition. As adaptivity has complex implications for the overall system, an explicit design of transition-enabled adaptive behavior is necessary and essential. So far, existing adaptive distributed systems lack a clear *separation of concerns* between the logic realizing adaptivity (the transition logic) and the actual application logic. A general concept to design and implement systems that allow for adaptivity in all key aspects is missing so far.

In this work, we propose a formal description of adaptivity through transitions and provide system developers with a sophisticated framework to describe and realize mechanism transitions in distributed systems. The approach allows mechanisms to be easily added over time to address new scenarios. Furthermore, the framework enables a clear separation of concerns between the transition and application logic. To identify the relevant functionality for the framework, two state-of-the-art systems (Bypass [14] and Transit [18]) targeting different application domains are analyzed. Even though both systems proved already that they highly benefit from adaptive behavior, a systematic approach to describe this behavior is missing so far. Based on the results, a first general design for the execution of transitions is derived and applied to the analyzed systems. By following the presented design, the mechanisms still define their application-specific interfaces. Additionally, transition-enabled mechanisms follow a common life cycle approach, managed by the framework. This allows us to (i) define *Elementary Transitions* between mechanism instances that can be performed during runtime and (ii) easily add new (specialized) mechanisms and transitions to an existing system. First proof-of-concept applications and initial evaluation results show that the approach is well-suited to describe and enable generic adaptivity in distributed systems by supporting mechanism transitions. As this work concentrates on the description and execution of transitions, the highly domain-specific adaptation decisions (based on performance models such as queuing models) are not discussed. However, our work poses a first step towards a generalization of the decision process by providing a unified description and handling of transitions in distributed systems.

The remainder of the paper is structured as follows: Section 2 presents the analysis of two existing adaptive systems and the derivation of requirements for the transition execution framework. The developed methodology, the derived life cycles and the framework is presented in Section 3 and discussed in Section 4. Subsequently, Section 5 presents related work and Section 6 concludes the paper.

2   Requirements Derivation

In this section, we analyze two state-of-the-art distributed systems and derive requirements for a transition framework.

2.1 Analysis of Bypass

Bypass [14] provides low-latency event dissemination for interactive mobile augmented reality games. In the targeted application scenario most events generated by mobile players are only relevant within a given area of interest around the player's current position. Therefore, once groups of nearby players are detected, the system adapts to local event delivery via ad hoc dissemination protocols. Depending on relevant environmental conditions (e.g. the group size), the local dissemination protocol is reconfigured or replaced. The original paper showed the benefit of adaptations to two local dissemination protocols: (i) a range-limited broadcast scheme and (ii) a probabilistic, gossip-like scheme. The authors further mention the possibility to switch between physical layer protocols, such as Wi-Fi ad hoc and Bluetooth. This leads to an architecture with a set of potential compositions as shown in Figure 1.

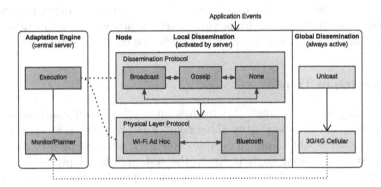

Fig. 1. Overview of Bypass and the possible transitions

The reconfigurations, i.e. the transitions between the local dissemination protocols, are not explicitly modeled in [14]. Instead, they are interweaved with the application logic and part of a predefined adaptation strategy at the cloud-based controller. Thus, no existing implementation for the recurring handling of transitions is used. This raises concerns as to how maintainable the adaptation implementation is, in particular how feasible it is to add new dissemination protocols, and how to implement the complex switch between these at runtime. We argue that a systematic methodology and a framework which supports this with well-defined interfaces for transition-enabled mechanisms significantly reduces the complexity of implementing and extending an adaptive distributed system.

Furthermore, the authors show that some nodes utilize different dissemination protocols. This causes approximately 40% of the overall message loss. We therefore propose an explicit life cycle management for the mechanisms involved in a transition. The coordinated life cycle has to enable a smooth handoff between two mechanisms, thereby reducing the amount of lost events caused by the transition itself.

The additionally possible transitions between Wi-Fi ad hoc and Bluetooth impose challenges to the existing transition handling. First of all, the establishment of the Bluetooth connection requires at least a short period of time, which causes an increased latency. Second, the establishment of the connections might fail for multiple reasons, which has to be compensated by the application. Switching between Wi-Fi and Bluetooth also affects the currently utilized dissemination protocol. Furthermore, sophisticated protocols require a specific physical layer protocol as they rely on assumptions regarding communication characteristics such as range or reliability. Therefore, we propose to build compositions of transitions to reflect dependencies, e.g. a transition between physical layer protocols might depend on a transition of the dissemination protocol.

As the aforementioned challenges are recurring for transitions in adaptive distributed systems, they should be handled by a transition framework to reduce the complexity. Depending on the mechanisms, state such as routes or neighbor tables are maintained that could benefit the target mechanism. Transferring state requires domain-specific knowledge, while conceptually being part of the transition logic. A transition framework needs to provide ways to utilize such knowledge in the transition handling to benefit the overall system.

2.2   Analysis of Transit

The streaming system Transit [18] realizes an overlay-based multicast service that adapts to a wide range of working conditions. For this, a main feature of the system is to flexibly adapt its overlay topology, which is used to distribute the video streams among participants in the system. The adaptivity is realized by different sets of *topology optimizations* (cf. Figure 2). These optimizations are usually executed in a distributed manner at the participants, also called peers in the following. While Transit includes several other mechanisms that realize adaptivity, including an extension [13] for network-layer multicast, in the following, we focus on overlay topology optimizations as they promise to have great potential for the adaptation considerations in this work.

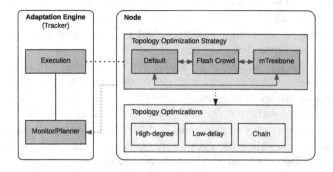

Fig. 2. Exemplary mechanisms and transitions in Transit

A challenging use case for topology adaptations are flash crowds, which are common to large-scale (video) streaming events. A large number of users needs to be quickly connected to the system. While in non-flash crowd times complex optimizations are reasonable to gradually improve the delivery process, here it is essential to quickly attach new peers to the topology and serve them with a low startup delay. One way to achieve this is to build topologies where many peers have free upload slots. Complex topology optimizations that could interfere with the attachment process should be disabled during the massive join phases of a flash crowd. Both can be achieved by defining topology optimizations strategies that define which optimizations are run. Therefore, as the topology adaptation logic is already modularized, this part of the system could greatly benefit from well-defined interfaces for transition-enabled components. Even though transitions between topology optimizations seem less complex as transitions in Bypass, a unified transition model which covers recurring challenges would improve the current systems and allow to build more complex systems easily.

3   Design and Description Methodology

3.1   Analysis of Transition Life Cycles

The systematic development of adaptive distributed systems requires abstractions. In the following, the *Elementary Transition* is introduced as the basic building block. Therefore, the *Life Cycle* of an elementary transition is defined based on the life cycle of the involved components. As the execution of a mechanism (e.g. Bypass's dissemination protocol) can be distributed over multiple nodes, we use *Components* as the smallest unit which is exchanged through a transition. A component implements all mechanism logic that is executed on a single node. Thus, the *Broadcast* components at multiple nodes together represent the *Broadcast Dissemination* mechanism in the distributed system.

To allow the application developer to abstract from the transition logic, a proxy [8] component is used instead of the actual component. This proxy intercepts all method invocations and forwards them to the currently active component instance. This enables a clear separation of concerns, as it strictly separates the application logic from the transition logic. The application only interacts with the proxy. A transition affects the inner workings of the proxy while leaving the reference to the proxy and the interface for the application unchanged. The proxy hides the exchange of the *Source* component with the *Target* component[1]. Additionally, the proxy instance ensures a thread-safe transition in a multithreaded environment. A transition between two components, for example, might not be executed while one thread is executing the source component (more precisely: while at least one method of the source component instance is part of a current execution stack). Similar problems might occur for application layer protocols, e.g. finishing a communication sequence before executing the transition. This follows the idea of *quiescence* as discussed by Pissias et al. [12].

---

[1] In the following, *component* is used instead of *component instance*.

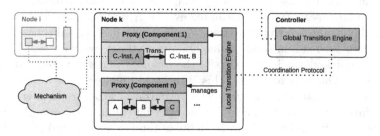

Fig. 3. Mechanisms comprise concurrently executed components on multiple nodes, each managed by a proxy instance

Figure 3 illustrates the overall architecture with multiple nodes, each executing components managed by proxies. The proxies are managed by the *Local Transition Engine*, which in turn is coordinated by the *Global Transition Engine*. Components on different nodes interact, thereby forming a mechanism.

Our analysis of the existing adaptive systems and their requirements lead to two kinds of elementary transitions, the *runrun* and the *flip transition*. Their most important difference is the life cycle and the parallel usage of the involved components. The flip transition does not execute both components in parallel and, thus, executes a hard switch, whereas the runrun transition smoothes the transition and executes both components in parallel for a short period of time, enabling a handover of, e.g., protocol state. Even though the runrun transition seems to be favorable, the flip transition is sometimes beneficial or even required due to resource constraints. For example, most mobile devices do not support the parallel usage of infrastructure Wi-Fi and Wi-Fi ad hoc, the parallel usage of Wi-Fi and LTE causes a higher energy consumption, and exclusive used software handles, e.g. established socket connections, cannot be shared. In the following, we discuss both transition types in detail.

Flip Transitions. The flip transition executes an abrupt switch between the source and target component. Figure 4 shows the life cycle of a component for such a transition. We model the life cycle as a mealy state machine which exchanges messages between the coordinating instance (the transition engine) and the component. Therefore, the state transitions of the state machine are annotated with the triggering messages (the input) which are sent to the component (above the bar) and the expected answer when the new state is reached (below the bar). For example, the transition engine signals an *init* to a newly created component. Once the component followed its internal initialization steps, it signals *finished* back to the transition engine leading to the *Initialized* state. During the initialization, the component executes preparation tasks such as allocating memory. The proxy ensures that methods of the component are not yet invoked. After the component has started successfully, and therefore can use the shared resources, it reaches the *Running* state and is used by the application.

Fig. 4. Single component life cycle of a *flip* transition

In case the component start fails, e.g. due to a network connection failure, it reaches the *Aborted* state. From the software engineering point of view, the actual *constructor* logic is distributed among the *init* and the *start* state transition.

Based on the component life cycle, we specify the life cycle of the flip transition (Figure 5). We denote messages exchanged with the components with an according prefix (*src:*, *trg:*). The *parent:*-prefix is used for message exchanges with the local transition engine as discussed later in this section. As the start of the target component may fail, the *Initialized* state has two outgoing state transitions. In case of a success, the flip transition finishes. Otherwise, the local transition engine decides, based on the specification of the application developer, if a new *recovery* component instance should be initialized or the transition fails. Please note that the details of these steps are skipped in the figure due to clarity.

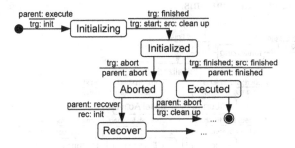

Fig. 5. Overall life cycle of a *flip* transition

Runrun Transitions. To reduce the performance degradation during the transition and allow a smooth transition, the runrun transition deactivates the source component when the target component is already running. This interweaving requires both components to be executed in parallel. The component life cycle reflects this with additional states (cf. Figure 6). The main difference is the state transition to the *Active* state and, thus, to the internal *Running* state. The *Active*-state additionally contains an *In Shutdown* state. Methods of the component can be executed during both internal active states. As the state transition to the *Running* state may fail, there is a state transition to the *Aborted* state as well. Additionally, the source component can be triggered to return to the *Running* state. In the *Active* state, the component can execute a state transition to the *Cleaned Up* state and clean up.

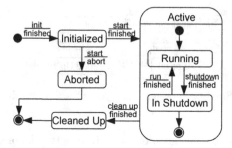

Fig. 6. Single component life cycle of a *runrun* transition

Based on this component life cycle, we define the life cycle of an elementary *runrun* transition (Figure 7). As the source component can be used in the *In Shutdown* state, the proxy can always forward method invocations, and therefore never blocks the application. This holds even for the time during the state transitions to the *Parallel Active* and the *Aborted* state. In case the start of the target component fails, the transition can always return to the source component. As the local transition engine coordinates the execution of a transition, it triggers the state transition to the *Clean up* and the *Rollback* state. Even though the component life cycle introduces a strict contract for the components, it allows easily integrating new mechanisms.

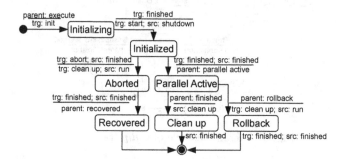

Fig. 7. Overall life cycle of a *runrun* transition

3.2   A Framework for Transition Description and Execution

Based on the two identified transition types and their life cycles, a systematic description and framework support for transitions is possible. In the following, we propose a transition description language, possible framework support, and suitable visualizations.

The transition description language allows to specify all available transitions and their affected components, as illustrated in Listing 1.1. As typical use cases have only a limited number of possible transitions, the exhaustive description of all transitions is without difficulty. Based on the described transitions, a *Global*

Transition Engine coordinates *Local Transition Engines* to execute distributed transitions. As both analyzed distributed systems have a centralized instance (the Cloud Server for Bypass and the Tracker for Transit), the assumption of a global transition engine is reasonable.

The coordination and synchronization of the proxies can be implemented efficiently. As in the two example applications multiple nodes execute the same transitions, the global transition engine does not require a huge and complex state machine (e.g. a Cartesian product of the involved life cycle states). Instead, a single state at the global transition engine can represent multiple states of the nodes. For scalability reasons, the global transition engine could use sub coordinators to handle the coordination messages. As this work focuses on the description and execution of transitions, a central coordinator is assumed. However, for future work, the methodology could be extended to support applications with a decentralized transition control.

The transition engines use the additional information from the transition description to control the transition execution. For example, the time the transition stays in the parallel active state (line 4), and the timeout which leads to a rollback of the transition (line 7) can be specified. In case a 'best effort' approach is sufficient, it is also possible to partly deactivate the transition coordination.

During both kinds of transition, state from the source component can be transferred to the target component. This state is represented by the references of the component and class instances which the source component transfers to the target component. As the transitions in the two analyzed systems both transfer this state in the life cycle state transition to the *Running* state, the framework makes this state transfer explicit and supports it in the transition description language (Listing 1.1 line 3). Components which only implement the stateless strategy pattern [8] do not require state transfer.

```
1   define elementary transition elTransition
2      from ComponentA to ComponentB type runrun
3      transfer state myStateVariable
4      parallel active for 1 minutes;
5   define parallel transition paraTransition
6      foreach A execute elemTransition
7      at least 90% timeout 2 minutes;
```

Listing 1.1. Example of the transition description language

Additional domain specific transition logic can be added in the host language and is invoked by the transition engine during the life cycle events. Such additional transition logic can, for example, be used to perform more complex state transfers involving the transformation of data. Even though both evaluated systems are based on Java, the presented approach is agnostic of the utilized programming language. The explicit notation of the transitions allows a clear separation between components and transitions and, this way, enables a systematic development of distributed adaptive systems. A framework which explicitly supports transitions between components and manages their execution provides multiple additional benefits. Besides development and debugging support, it can, for example, monitor and ensure that only one transition per proxy instance is executed at the same time, and started transitions finally terminate.

Traditionally, there are two viewpoints on systems, the structural and the behavioral [9]. The composition of components describes structural properties, whereas the execution of a transition is behavior which changes the structure. We propose a combined view as a class diagram (Figure 8). The ternary association connects the source and the target component with the specific transition logic. The stereotypes *TransitionEnabled* and *TransitionLogic* are resolved to implementations of the corresponding interfaces. The transferred state (more precisely, the transferred references to other objects) is visualized as well.

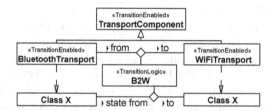

Fig. 8. UML visualization of transitions and the composition variability of components

4   Discussion

To assess the impact of the proposed design methodology, the presented concepts were applied on both systems. For the existing transitions between local dissemination protocols in Bypass, the new version which leverages the framework reduces the transition specific lines of code to roughly 20% of the original code. This greatly reduces the complexity of the implementation. Even more important, the transition-specific source code is no longer part of the application logic but instead encapsulated by the transition engine, providing separation of concerns. Additionally, this reduces the error probability, as proved transition handling code is reused. In addition to porting Bypass to our framework, we added new component that encapsulate the physical layer protocols as proposed by the authors. Therefore, the existing interaction via Wi-Fi ad hoc was realized as a component instance as shown in Figure 1. Additionally, we added a component instance that enables local communication via Bluetooth and defined a runrun transition between both instances (cf. Listing 1.2).

Our implementations show that Bypass benefits from the concept of parallel and sequential transitions. Switching the local dissemination protocol after the physical protocol switched successfully, is defined as a sequential transition (Listing 1.2), composed of two elementary transitions. In case the connection setup using Bluetooth fails, the overall transition returns to a well-defined system state. Considering the life cycle of a *runrun* transition (Figure 7), the transition enters the *Aborted* state and consequently recovers by just continuing to use Wi-Fi as active component instance. Composing transitions out of elementary transitions is straight forward with the presented framework, as they can easily be described in the transition description language. Thereby, common pitfalls such as illegal combinations or undefined transitions are detected early. The abstraction of the underlying life cycle enables more complex combinations. For future work, it is interesting to combine constraints on the possible component compositions and properties of the compositions, e.g. as proposed by [7], to further support the developer, e.g. verify legal transitions.

```
1   define elementary transition WiFi2BT
2       from WiFiAdHoc to Bluetooth type runrun;
3   define elementary transition Gossip2BC
4       from Gossip to Broadcast type runrun;
5   define sequential transition SeqTrans (WiFi2BT, Gossip2BC);
```

Listing 1.2. An elementary transition from Wi-Fi to Bluetooth composed with a subsequent dissemination protocol transition

Applying the concept to transitions between topology optimization strategies in Transit was possible in a straightforward manner with very localized changes at the respective components. As an extension, the concept of so called *Optimization Providers* was introduced to bundle sets of currently active topology optimizations. The transition framework was then used to allow for *flip* transitions between different provider implementations. As topology optimizations and their execution are decoupled by design, there was no need to consider optimizations and providers that are active in a parallel manner. Providers that reuse topology optimization instances (in case two providers include similar optimizations) benefit from the automatic state transfer of the framework. As a side effect, the approach showed to be very helpful to rapidly define and evaluate new optimization combinations for new scenarios. With the legacy implementation, this requires large changes to various parts of the optimization implementations, thus heavily mixing adaptation and application behavior.

5   Related Work

Compositional adaptation [11] is an established concept for adaptive systems. Many systems [5, 15, 16] leverage proxies to enable transparent dynamic composition for the application or extend the host language to enable adaptive behavior [10]. Sadjadi et al. [15] use this concept for communication systems and adapt between different forward error correction schemes in the network. However, these systems lack a model for the actual transition life cycle and state transfer. Additionally, they do not provide abstractions for multiple (parallel or sequential) transitions, even though their proxies can be distributed.

Many component-based systems benefit from an explicit component life cycle. In OSGi [2], for example, bundles and their components follow a clear life cycle. This enables OSGi to install, update, remove, start, and stop components at runtime without stopping the system. The different components are loosely coupled using service bindings. Even though our presented component life cycle is inspired by the bundle life cycle in OSGi, we consequently enhance this concept to model the life cycle of *transitions between components* in distributed environments. This reduces the switching costs and allows transfer state and composed transitions. The handling of service bindings is hidden by the proxies.

IBM proposes the MAPE-K concept for autonomic control loops [1]. In this model, the *Autonomic Manager* manages the tasks *monitor, analyze, plan,* and *execute* as well as the globally shared *knowledge. Effectors* perform changes on *Managed Elements*, which represent any adaptive software/hardware component. Our proxies represent a special of managed element with clearly modeled transition capabilities. The transition description is globally shared knowledge.

Ferreira et al. [6] developed A-OSGi to support the construction of autonomic OSGi-based applications. Therefore, they integrate the MAPE-K approach into OSGi. Concentrating on the monitoring, the actual adaptations are simple service binding changes, bundle starts, or changes of service properties. A detailed concept for more complex component exchanges and state transfer is missing.

The knowledge about valid configurations and component compositions is important to deal with reconfiguration consistency. Batista et al. [3], for example, model this and use it to check reconfigurations, but do not investigate the actual transitions which lead to these configurations. As our current solution concentrates on the description and the life cycle of transitions, integration of both approaches might allow to reason about consistent and legal transitions.

Coulson et al. [4] propose a middleware approach for reconfigurable distributed systems. The middleware is utilized in the publish/subscribe system GREEN [17] to enable reconfiguration of multiple publish/subscribe-specific components. However, they do not provide a clear description of the reconfiguration possibilities. Transitions in between configurations and implications such as state transfer and life cycle management are not detailed.

6   Conclusion and Future Work

In this paper, we identified recurring requirements to handle adaptive behavior in distributed systems. Based on this, we proposed a framework which supports two transition life cycles and provides a clear abstraction of the underlying complex transition logic. The concept was applied to two example systems to practically evaluate its benefits. In both cases, the approach leads to less complex realizations of adaptivity and allows new mechanisms to be integrated easily.

For future work, we consider to leverage the proposed concept and methodology to design and study a new class of highly adaptive distributed systems that were not feasible so far. While the proposed approach builds the foundation for this, additional support for more dependencies between transitions and according coordination strategies, e.g. a decentralized coordination, need to be developed as next steps.

Acknowledgments. This work has been funded by the German Research Foundation (DFG) within the Collaborative Research Center (CRC) 1053 – MAKI.

References

1. An Architectural Blueprint for Autonomic Computing. Tech. rep. IBM (2003)
2. OSGi Service Platform Core Specification (2007)
3. Batista, T.V., Joolia, A., Coulson, G.: Managing Dynamic Reconfiguration in Component-Based Systems. In: Morrison, R., Oquendo, F. (eds.) EWSA 2005. LNCS, vol. 3527, pp. 1–17. Springer, Heidelberg (2005)
4. Coulson, G., Blair, G.S., Clarke, M., Parlavantzas, N.: The Design of a Configurable and Reconfigurable Middleware Platform. Distributed Computing 15(2) (2002)
5. Felber, P., Garbinato, B., Guerraoui, R.: Towards reliable CORBA: Integration vs. service approach. Tech. rep. dpunkt-Verlag (1997)
6. Ferreira, J., Leitão, J., Rodrigues, L.: A-OSGi: A Framework to Support the Construction of Autonomic OSGi-Based Applications. In: Vasilakos, A.V., Beraldi, R., Friedman, R., Mamei, M. (eds.) Autonomics 2009. LNICST, vol. 23, pp. 1–16. Springer, Heidelberg (2010)
7. Frömmgen, A., Lehn, M., Buchmann, A.: A property description framework for composable software. In: Avgeriou, P., Zdun, U. (eds.) ECSA 2014. LNCS, vol. 8627, pp. 267–282. Springer, Heidelberg (2014)
8. Gamma, E., Helm, R., Johnson, R., Vlissides, J.: Design Patterns: Elements of Reusable Object-oriented Software. Pearson (1994)
9. Hilliard, R.: Recommended Practice for Architectural Description of Software-intensive Systems. IEEE Std. 1471-2000 (2000)
10. Kasten, E., McKinley, P., Sadjadi, S., Stirewalt, R.: Separating Introspection and Interception to Support Metamorphic Distributed Systems. In: Distributed Computing Systems Workshops (2002)
11. McKinley, P.K., Sadjadi, S.M., Kasten, E.P., Cheng, B.H.C.: Composing Adaptive Software. Computer 37(7) (July 2004)
12. Pissias, P., Coulson, G.: Framework for Quiescence Management in Support of Reconfigurable Multi-threaded Component-based Systems. IET Software 2(4) (2008)
13. Rückert, J., Blendin, J., Hausheer, D.: Software-Defined Multicast for Over-the-Top and Overlay-based Live Streaming in ISP Networks. Springer JNSM, Special Issue on Management of Software-defined Networks (2014)
14. Richerzhagen, B., Stingl, D., Hans, R., Groß, C., Steinmetz, R.: Bypassing the Cloud: Peer-assisted Event Dissemination for Augmented Reality Games. In: Proc. P2P. IEEE (2014)
15. Sadjadi, S.M., McKinley, P.K., Kasten, E.P., Zhou, Z.: MetaSockets: Design and Operation of Runtime Reconfigurable Communication Services: Experiences with Auto-adaptive and Reconfigurable Systems. Softw. Pract. Exper. 36(11-12) (2006)
16. Sadjadi, S.M., McKinley, P.K.: ACT: An Adaptive CORBA Template to Support Unanticipated Adaptation. In: Distributed Computing Systems. IEEE (2004)
17. Sivaharan, T., Blair, G.S., Coulson, G.: GREEN: A Configurable and Re-configurable Publish-Subscribe Middleware for Pervasive Computing. In: Meersman, R., Tari, Z. (eds.) OTM 2005. LNCS, vol. 3760, pp. 732–749. Springer, Heidelberg (2005)
18. Wichtlhuber, M., Richerzhagen, B., Rückert, J., Hausheer, D.: TRANSIT: Supporting Transitions in Peer-to-Peer Live Video Streaming. In: IFIP NETWORKING (2014)

A Network-Driven Multi-Access-Point Load-Balancing Algorithm for Large-Scale Public Hotspots

Patrick Bosch$^{(\boxtimes)}$, Bart Braem, and Steven Latré

University of Antwerp - iMinds, Department of Mathematics and Computer Science
Middelheimlaan 1, B-2020 Antwerp, Belgium
{patrick.bosch,bart.braem,steven.latre}@uantwerpen.be

Abstract. Wireless networks are getting more and more popular and are a basic part of our life with the daily use of smartphones. Users expect high quality connectivity even in public spaces where a high number of clients connect to a limited spectrum on a geographically small area. Therefore, large-scale, high density wireless networks, like they are present at events, are getting more common, but provide a serious resource allocation challenge. Thousands of clients want to connect to a network consisting of multiple APs and a limited spectrum, while all of them should receive a decent connection quality, throughput and delay. Therefore, none of the APs should be overloaded, so that they can provide service for each connected client. The *IEEE 802.11* standard stipulates that the client makes the decision to which AP to connect to. In high-density networks, the individual decision of the client can lead to an AP overload and oscillations in AP association as a client typically has limited information about the network performance and does not collaborate with other clients in taking its decision. This provides unwanted behaviour for load-balancing, as there is no control over the clients. Therefore, we present a method where the APs get control over the client and realise load balancing in such a network. The AP evaluates through a score if the client can connect and, if the client is connected, checks regularly if it is the best option for the client.

1 Introduction

With the rise of smartphones, users expect to be always connected to the Internet. Besides 3G and 4G in outside areas, we have Wi-Fi at home, at work, in public spaces or at events. Because of the increasing demand for broadband connectivity, we can see an increase in deployment of public hotspots. For example, cities offer free Wi-Fi in public areas. The architecture of those hotspots consists of multiple access points (APs). Users expect wireless broadband connectivity with the same quality as at home in these locations. The main challenge for public hotspots is the number of users that use the hotspots and the resulting high density of users. Each AP has only a limited spectrum available, which make proper management techniques necessary to avoid low quality connections with very little bandwidth or even losing the connection.

© IFIP International Federation for Information Processing 2015
S. Latré et al. (Eds.): AIMS 2015, LNCS 9122, pp. 30–42, 2015.
DOI: 10.1007/978-3-319-20034-7_3

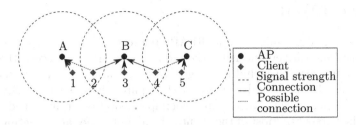

Fig. 1. Possibility of client distribution among APs. Client 2 and 4 have two possible APs each. Client 2 can connect to AP A and B and client 4 to AP B and C.

In *IEEE 802.11*, further mentioned as Wi-Fi, a client is free to choose an AP. The standard selection criterion to choose an AP is the received signal strength indication (RSSI) of said AP. The exact decision is implementation dependent, but usually a client has a list of all available APs and tries to connect to the one with the strongest signal. This can lead to a degradation of the connection quality on an AP due to overload, if most of the clients try to connect to the same AP. Only the AP has knowledge about the number of clients connected to it and how much bandwidth is already consumed. If an AP gets overloaded, the overall throughput and throughput per client drastically decreases, resulting in a bad connection for the client. To avoid this, we need load-balancing to distribute the clients evenly among all available APs.

There are two main approaches to balance the load in such a system. Either a client-driven approach, where the selection criterion of the client is changed, or a network-driven approach, where the AP does the balancing. There are several proposals that are targeting the client and increase throughput through a new selection process [2] [9] [6] [15] [5] [11] [8]. However, this assumes we have control over the client (e.g., by ways of a modified MAC protocol), which is normally not the case. It is more sensible to assume that we cannot change the client and concentrate on the AP to achieve a balanced load.

In this article we present a network-driven load-balancing approach that is able to actively influence clients to connect to the best AP. The contributions of this paper are three-fold. First, we provide a distributed load-balancing algorithm that evaluates the association of the clients via a score computation. Second, we introduce a new way for APs to exchange information, so every AP can compute the score of its neighbours for a client. Third, we provide a way to encourage clients to connect to a more advantageous AP. We use existing standards to control where a client can connect and try to move clients if the score suggests this, making the procedure completely transparent for the mobile device. To demonstrate the possibilities of our algorithm, we set up a simulation in *ns-3* and will provide the results.

The remainder of this article is structured as follows. In Section 2 we discuss previous work. Following in Section 3, we state the problem formally. The algorithm is explained in Section 4 and the performance is evaluated in Section 5. Finally, we conclude in Section 6.

2   Related Work

Load-balancing algorithms for a multi-AP architecture can be organised in two main areas: client-driven and network-driven. As the names suggest, the client-driven driven approach includes changes in the client (e.g., through the MAC protocol) and the network-driven approach requires changes to the network infrastructure (i.e., by changing the protocol implementation of the provided large-scale public hotspots). Most of the client-driven approaches are targeting the selection mechanism of the client and propose a new one that offers load-balancing and increases performance. In practice, a network infrastructure provider typically wants to optimise the performance of the large-scale public hotspot he provides. As he cannot alter clients, an approach that requires the client to change is not possible.

As multi-AP architectures are becoming more common, the *IEEE 802.11* standards committee has also investigated roaming between APs by proposing several extensions to the *IEEE 802.11* standard. *IEEE 802.11-2012* includes the standards previously known as *IEEE 802.11k*, *r* and *v*, which are targeting roaming and information gathering [1] [10]. *IEEE 802.11v* offers the possibility for the AP to suggest a client to move to another AP, but it is still the client, which decides if it will follow the suggestion. These standards may seem very attractive at first, but are not mandatory for a vendor to implement and are not widely used today. Depending on the acceptance of the vendors, these may be a possibility in the future.

Because of the poor acceptance by vendors of roaming-based amendments to *IEEE 802.11*, new load-balancing algorithms are currently an open research challenge in literature. In the default *IEEE 802.11* standard family, the RSSI is the standard selection method for a client. This method is not ideal, because it does not consider the actual load on the AP or how many clients are connected to it. Therefore new selection criteria regarding load balancing were proposed. One possibility is to target the data rate. A new client will evaluate the data rate, while considering the data rate of already connected clients. Additional to modifications on the client, changes to the AP are also necessary to provide more information to the client [2]. Another possibility is to estimate the bandwidth that will be available for the client by sending control frames [9]. Based on that, the client then decides which AP to connect to. Regarding its own throughput and not to reduce the throughput of other clients, a decentralised algorithm is proposed, where each station can decide for itself which AP to connect to [6]. Estimating both, downstream and upstream, a decision is made and the client can connect to the best possible AP [15]. The approach can also be solved by forming zones of devices that are supported by the same set of APs [5]. The client estimates the bit rate of all APs in the zones and selects the one, which can provide enough bandwidth for it. There is also an approach, which implements a whole system that checks out every AP in its vicinity and tests the performance for each network, to find out the best AP to associate with [11]. There are also approaches with less changes to the client [8]. A new field to the beacon message is added, which provides more information for the client. The problem with all of these approaches, however, is that they completely rely on the support of the client. While this might work for an individual client, in a large-scale public hotspot, it is not realistic to assume a wide adoption of one algorithm. As such, all these algorithms fail in providing a global network optimisation across APs.

The latter calls for more network-driven approaches. One such approach was proposed by Scully et al. [12]. There, a centralised genetic algorithm is presented that can distribute the clients among the APs. However, while the decision is calculated, it does not offer a solution as how to influence the client to connect to the correct AP and the algorithm can not make a decision immediately. In this paper, we provide a way to influence these clients and present our own algorithm for making the decision.

To the best of our knowledge, our algorithm is the first to propose a network-driven solution with direct influence on the clients and without any support of the client itself.

3   Problem Statement

The multi-AP load-balancing algorithm can be formulated as follows. We define a multi-AP architecture with a set of APs $A = \{1, ..., n\}$, which are set up in infrastructure mode and connected via wire. The APs are deployed in such a way that their coverage areas are overlapping (see Figure 1). Further, we have a set of clients $C = \{1, ..., m\}$, with a size of several thousands. The clients can move around freely in a restricted area that is limited in size. C can be divided into two subsets, $MC = \{1, ..., k\}$ and $NMC = \{k+1, ..., m\}$, according to the behaviour of the clients. MC is the set of *movable clients* whereas NMC is the set of *non-movable clients*. A *movable client* is defined as a client that can be moved to another AP and accordingly a *non-movable client* is defined as a client that cannot be moved to another AP, which means it will stick to the one to which it is connected to and tries to reconnect there. This is an implementation dependent behaviour, as it is not standardised how a client should behave in this situation. Obviously, a client cannot be both, therefore, $MC \cap NMC$. The goal is to have a mapping $C {\rightarrow} A$, so that all m clients are connected, but every individual client is only connected to one and only one of the APs. This is to be done in such a way that the overall throughput as well as the bandwidth usage and the bandwidth per client is maximised. Additionally to the assignment, it also has to be executed. That is to say, we need a way to encourage clients to connect to the AP that is the best choice for the client and therefore for the network itself. This has to be done without any change to the client.

One possible application would be a public event like a concert. At events, we have a large amount of people, usually several thousands, which are concentrated on a comparatively small area. This results in the aforementioned high density of clients, as well as the mobility of the clients. Visitors of such events tend to move around in the area. The organiser of the event wants to provide additional services through Wi-Fi to enhance the experience of the visitors. Therefore, he places APs throughout the area and the visitors have access to the Wi-Fi network. We cannot assume that visitors will be evenly distributed. It is more realistic to assume that there will be some areas with higher density and some areas with lower density. APs in higher density areas need to be relieved of too much burden by distributing the clients to other APs. We can also not assume access to client devices, as well as similar behaviour from device to device. We can only assume that clients support the mandatory features of the *IEEE 802.11* standard. Therefore, we can only use standardised messages when we communicate with the client.

4 Network-Driven Multi-AP Load-Balancing

The main idea of the approach is a decentralised score computation algorithm, which has the advantage that we can react faster to the requests of a client, which is necessary if we consider the amount of clients that will try to connect Each AP computes a score for a client when it tries to connect to the AP, as depicted in Figure 2. Beside the computation of its own score, the AP has means to compute the score for its neighbours too. If the AP has the best score, it accepts the client, otherwise it rejects the client and informs the neighbour with the best score. To realise the score computation for neighbouring APs, information needs to be exchanged between the APs. To realise this, we introduce a *neighbour update*. This allows the APs to exchange information about their status. We also consider *NMCs* insofar that we let them connect if they tried more than twice to reconnect. This reduces overall performance, but we need to guarantee connectivity for every client. The score itself is recomputed periodically to check if a client can have a better AP. If this is the case then the client is encouraged to move to the new AP.

4.1 Score Computation

The computation of the score is based on parameters that are broadcasted with the *neighbour update*. We will explain this mechanism later on. The parameters can be arranged in groups according to their interconnectivity. At first we have a group of network related parameters that inform us about the performance of the network, seen from each AP and individual for the AP, which are: {*bandwidth usage (BU), bandwidth per client (BPC), throughput (T)*}. Then we have AP related parameters that give us information about the performance of the AP. These consist of: {*CPU utilisation (CPU), number of clients (NC) (active (NCA), idle (NCI)), supported and actual data rate (SDR, ADR), number of NMC (NON)*}. And at last, we have environment related parameters, which include: {*signal to noise ratio (SNR), location of client and AP (L_c, L_{ap})*}.

All of the information is gathered on each AP. For the purpose of this paper, we will focus on the most important parameters. These encompass the full group of network related parameters {*bandwidth usage, bandwidth per client, throughput*}, part of the AP related parameters {*number of clients (active, idle), number of NMC*} as well as part of the environment parameters {*location of client and AP*} from which we calculate the distance D of the client to the AP.

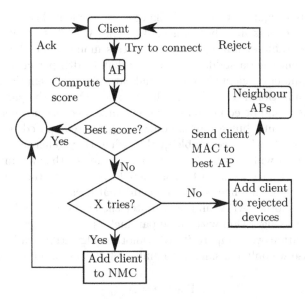

Fig. 2. Client tries to connect to AP. AP computes score to check if the client is allowed to connect and either lets it connect or denies the connection.

We want a fast computation of the score, therefore we prioritise performance above accuracy. To make the comparison of scores easier, we want a single score, but we cannot neglect the dependency of the parameters on to each other. A high number of clients on an AP does not necessarily imply bad performance. If only a very small amount of clients is active and do not need a lot of bandwidth, there is plenty of bandwidth still available. On the other hand, if there are several APs with low bandwidth usage, we still need a way to decide which one is most fitting. In this case the number of connected clients will get important again.

As a general formula for the computation, based on empirical observations, we use

$$\text{AP score} = (NC \times D \times T \times BU \times (1/BPC)) + NC \times D \qquad (1)$$

where we choose the AP with the lowest score. In early simulations, we realised that the score can fluctuate very fast and that some clients could not connect due to that. Therefore, we introduced a smoothing interval. If the AP is not the best, but within the interval, then the AP will accept the client nevertheless. Through tests, we determined that 20% is a satisfiable value which prevents fluctuation. Different parameters have a different impact on the score and regarding them exclusively is not sufficient. We weight distance, number of clients and bandwidth per client higher than the others due to their direct influence on the quality of the connection for a client. The bandwidth per client has a high weight because it fulfils mainly two roles. First, it indicates the possible performance for the client on the AP and second it indicates an estimate of the impact on the performance for the client if the throughput is low. Although there is little to no throughput right now, it could change any moment, because a relatively high amount of clients may be connected to the AP. These connected clients could generate traffic at any time and from this moment on, the AP is a bad choice. To prevent such a sudden impact, the bandwidth per client indicator is of help. The number of clients is another indicator for this scenario, which is the reason for the additional use of it and the distance. One of the parameters, like the throughput, could be equal to zero, for example, because no client is sending anything at that time, but a high amount of clients, compared to the amount of clients serviceable with acceptable quality when they generate traffic, is connected. The clients will then be distributed according to the amount of them on each AP. The distance needs to be considered even when other information is not available, because a longer distance means that it can reduce the bit rate for the AP or that another AP would be a better choice, because it is closer to the client. We call the algorithm with these parameters the *advanced* one.

In the evaluation we compare it with another algorithm, called the *simple* one. In this case we only consider the number of clients on an AP to distribute the clients.

$$\text{AP score} = NC \tag{2}$$

We do not consider any other factor, like throughput or bandwidth per client, in the simple algorithm.

4.2   Client Distribution

The computation is done for each client once when it tries to connect to the AP during the authentication phase. The algorithm itself is illustrated in Figure 2. First, the aforementioned score is computed. Based on this score, the client is then either rejected or accepted. If it is rejected, the best AP will be informed to accept the client immediately, so that the AP does not need to compute the score again. If two APs have the same score, both will be notified and the one where the client tries to connect first accepts the client. We also remember the clients that tried to connect for a time. If the client is trying more than two times to connect to the AP in a short time frame, then it means it is a *NMC*. This client is accepted and marked as such.

As clients move around over time, there might be a better AP to which they should connect. Therefore, a periodic recomputation of the score for each client is done to make sure that the AP is still the best one for the client and that the AP itself does not get cluttered with clients that have a better option. The process is presented in Figure 3. If the client is not active right now, if it does not send traffic, the client will be removed from the AP and prevented to connect to it again. The client will only be prevented to connect again for a specific amount of time, after that it can connect to that AP again. If for some reason the AP becomes the best choice again within that amount of time, the client will not be prevented to connect, because another AP informed that AP that it should let the client connect. If the client is active, it will not be removed, but as soon as it gets inactive, the AP will remove it, so that it can connect to

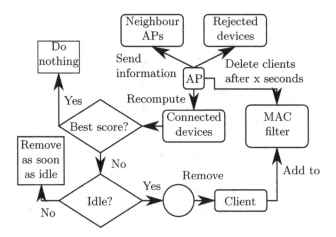

Fig. 3. The AP sends periodic updates to its neighbours and recomputes the score for each connected client

another AP. Through the recomputation, clients are moved around to increase the performance of the AP, but also the performance of the client, because the new AP can offer it a better connection.

Another periodic mechanism is the *neighbour update*. We use it to keep the information on an AP about its neighbours in sync. To be sure to have the same score for each AP-client combination on every AP, we use on each AP only the information that was last received, respectively sent. The update itself is realised with UDP packets. Every AP encodes the information it has to sent into the payload and sends the packet via broadcast in the wired sub-network. The information itself is represented as comma separated values. The clients do not come in contact with it, as it is not broadcasted in the wireless medium. By sending it through the wire the information is available for every AP and they can get the best score available for a client. Additionally to the periodic sending of updates, there is also the possibility to send updates on demand. This is used to inform another AP that it is the best option for a specific client, so that it can immediately accept the client when it tries to connect without computing a score.

4.3 Client Encouragement

To enforce our distribution, we encourage clients to connect to another AP and use only standardised mechanisms for that, so that we do not have to make any changes on the client.

We are using four possibilities that an AP has according to the standard, which are *MAC filter, not answering probe requests, reject at authentication* and *deauthentication.*

The first three are used to prevent a client from connecting to an AP. The rejection at the time of the authentication is used at the time when the client

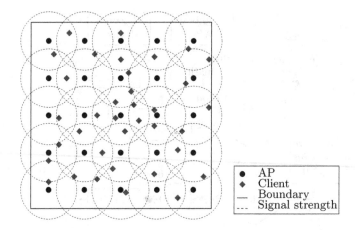

Fig. 4. Topology of simulation. We have 25 distributed APs and randomly distributed and randomly moving clients.

tries to connect for the first time on that AP or enough time has passed that the MAC filter was already removed. The filter is removed after 3 seconds. The MAC filter denies the client to connect to the AP again and the denial of a probe response encourages the client to search for another AP. If the client does not receive a probe response, it will assume that the old AP is not there anymore. Both of those are used when a client was removed from the AP to prevent that the client connects again. The deauthentication is only used to remove a client from the AP and encourage it to choose another AP. After the deauthentication, a MAC filter is used to prevent the client to connect again.

5   Performance Evaluation

5.1   Evaluation Environment

For the evaluation, we set up an *ns-3* simulation. We implemented the algorithm for the APs according to the description above and chose a neighbour update interval of 100 ms. The topology itself is described in Figure 4. 25 APs are evenly distributed in the restricted area of 100 to 100 meters. Their coverage overlaps, so a client can always connect. We used the Wi-Fi standard *IEEE 802.11g* due to the fact that it is the most stable implementation in *ns-3*. The standard propagation model was used with an additional maximum range of 28 meters. We set up the simulation with 500 clients to demonstrate our algorithm. All the clients move around randomly, but they can only move around in the restricted area to achieve a high density of clients at all times. The initial distribution of the clients is according to the random allocation model of the simulator. As a mobility model we chose the random walk model. Traffic is produced by several servers, which send to the clients, which can be seen as a streaming of a video

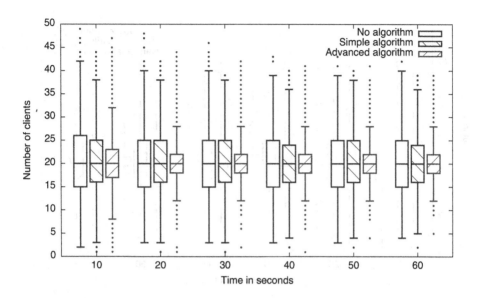

Fig. 5. Distribution of the number of clients over time, captured every 10 seconds. Outliers with the same value are grouped together, their percentage is below 2%.

for example. This is realised through UDP applications with a constant bit rate of 0.25 Mbit/s for each client. The overall simulation time was 70 seconds. The start of the search for an AP for the clients was randomly triggered within the first 5 seconds, to relax the burst a bit and get a more realistic situation. The applications too, were not started immediately, but with 3 ms delay between each other. The APs in this simulation do not have any mechanisms to adapt their settings, like transmission power, transmission range, to avoid collisions and congestion, like some professional APs have. Therefore we chose a setting where we do not have channel saturation, but are close to it. To get meaningful results, we did run the simulation 100 times with different seeds, resulting in 2500 samples for each time stamp. We measured everything directly on the AP.

We will compare our algorithm with the state of the art method, which is basically no control, and the simple algorithm that just considers the number of clients on an AP. We compare the distribution of the clients amongst the APs as well as the throughput distribution amongst the APs.

5.2   Results Description

In all graphs, the whiskers mark the 1.5 interquartile range, while the outliers mark the points outside of that range. Their percentage is very low in each graph and are statistically not significant. Therefore, we will not regard those in our further analysis.

Figure 5 illustrates the evolution of the distribution of clients on all APs for all three scenarios, depicted every 10 seconds. The recomputation is done every 15

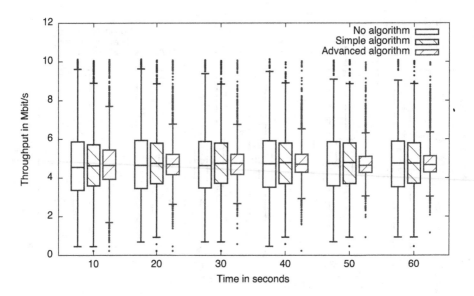

Fig. 6. The distribution of the throughput over time, captured every 10 seconds. Outliers with the same value are grouped together, their percentage is below 1%.

seconds and the clients are moved to another AP and get more evenly distributed with the advanced algorithm than with the other two. The deviation over time is getting lower, until it reaches a stable distribution. Compared to the other two, the advanced algorithm can keep this deviation due to the recomputation and the more complex score computation. The simple algorithm also has an advantage over the state of the art method, as it considers the number of clients as a criterion, but it can not compete with the advanced one. The overall number of clients is stable over all three algorithms, which means all clients are assigned to an AP and can use the connection for services. Overall, the load-balancing algorithms distribute the clients more evenly, where the advanced one is the best amongst them, followed by the simple one and at last the state of the art method.

In Figure 6 we can see the distribution of the throughput of every AP. Similar to the number of clients, the throughput is more evenly distributed with the advanced algorithm than with no algorithm or the simple one. We can see that the minimum value of the throughput is higher for the advanced algorithm due to the better distribution of the clients. The maximum value on the other hand is a bit lower, due to the fact that less clients are connected. Again, the deviation, compared to the other two, is lower and can be kept during the whole time. This means, that there is still throughput available on each AP and the clients experience a better connection with lesser delay and lesser packet loss, by reason of a lesser amount of clients competing for air time.

The better distribution of the number of clients and throughput amongst the APs allows for further capacities on each access point for the advanced algorithm. On the other hand, if we have no algorithm, some APs are already overloaded or close to it, while others still have capacity. If the number of clients on the APs, which are close to being overloaded, would increase, they can not serve them anymore with an acceptable quality, while the APs with the advanced algorithm still can, because they have spare capacity on each one. In the context of moving clients, the advanced one can handle those more easily as it actively moves them to another AP, while the clients stick to the AP for the state of the art method. This leads to a degeneration of experience for clients over time. The advanced algorithm can avoid this degeneration with the recomputation.

Overall, the simple algorithm does not far as good as the advanced one, because it considers less parameters. But it can still show an improvement over the algorithm with no control. The advanced one considers more parameters and can improve the performance of the network significantly more. The state of the art method can not compete with both of them and shows worse network performance and therefore a worse experience for the client.

6 Conclusion and Future Work

In this paper, we presented a network-driven approach that can improve the performance of the network, regarding throughput distribution and distribution of clients, without any change on the clients. The control over the decisions where a client is connected, is transferred to the AP. The information exchange between the APs allows for a better view on the network and can be used on each AP to independently decide which is the best AP for a client. The decision is enforced through the use of standardised methods.

As future work, our approach can be combined with other methods, such as cell breathing to allow for further improvement [3] [7]. If the standards *IEEE 802.11k/r/v* become more commonly implemented, these can also be used [1] [10]. A crowd movement model, as well as more realistic traffic generation can be added. The placement of the APs can also be researched, as realistic settings do not always allow for evenly distributed APs. As the proposed algorithm might need more messages from clients, the impact on the battery level can be researched.

Acknowledgements. Part of this work has been funded by the iFEST project, cofunded by iMinds, a digital research institute founded by the Flemish Government. Project partners are PlayPass, ID&T, Telenet, Argus Labs, Cozmos and Sendrato, with project support from IWT.

References

1. IEEE Standard for Information technology–Telecommunications and information exchange between systems Local and metropolitan area networks–Specific requirements Part 11: Wireless LAN Medium Access Control (MAC) and Physical Layer (PHY) Specifications. IEEE Std 802.11-2012 (Revision of IEEE Std 802.11-2007), pp. 1–2793 (2012)

2. Abusubaih, M., Wiethoelter, S., Gross, J., Wolisz, A.: A New Access Point Selection Policy for Multi-rate IEEE 802.11 WLANs. Int. J. Parallel Emerg. Distrib. Syst. 23, 291–307 (2008)
3. Bahl, P.V., Hajiaghayi, M.T., Jain, K., Mirrokni, S.V., Qiu, L., Saberi, A.: Cell Breathing in Wireless LANs: Algorithms and Evaluation. IEEE Transactions on Mobile Computing 6, 164–178 (2007)
4. Bejerano, Y., Han, S.J., Li, L.: Fairness and load balancing in wireless lans using association control. IEEE/ACM Transactions on Networking 15, 560–573 (2007)
5. Dandapat, S., Mitra, B., Choudhury, R., Ganguly, N.: Smart Association Control in Wireless Mobile Environment Using Max-Flow. IEEE Transactions on Network and Service Management 9, 73–86 (2012)
6. Fukuda, Y., Abe, T., Oie, Y.: Decentralized access point selection architecture for wireless LANs. In: Wireless Telecommunications Symposium, pp. 137–145 (2004)
7. Garcia, E., Vidal, R., Paradells, J.: Cooperative load balancing in IEEE 802.11 networks with cell breathing. In: IEEE Symposium on Computers and Communications, ISCC 2008, pp. 1133–1140 (2008)
8. Gong, H., Kim, J.: Dynamic load balancing through association control of mobile users in WiFi networks. IEEE Transactions on Consumer Electronics 54, 342–348 (2008)
9. Lee, H., Kim, S., Lee, O., Choi, S., Lee, S.J.: Available Bandwidth-based Association in IEEE 802.11 Wireless LANs. In: Proceedings of the 11th International Symposium on Modeling, Analysis and Simulation of Wireless and Mobile Systems, MSWiM 2008, pp. 132–139. ACM, New York (2008)
10. Machań, P., Wozniak, J.: On the fast BSS transition algorithms in the IEEE 802.11r local area wireless networks. Telecommunication Systems 52, 2713–2720 (2013)
11. Nicholson, A.J., Chawathe, Y., Chen, M.Y., Noble, B.D., Wetherall, D.: Improved Access Point Selection. In: Proceedings of the 4th International Conference on Mobile Systems, Applications and Services, MobiSys 2006, pp. 233–245. ACM, New York (2006)
12. Scully, T., Brown, K.: Wireless LAN Load-Balancing with Genetic Algorithms. In: Allen, T., Ellis, R., Petridis, M. (eds.) Applications and Innovations in Intelligent Systems XVI, pp. 3–16. Springer, London (2009)
13. Siris, V., Evaggelatou, D.: Access point selection for improving throughput fairness in wireless lans. In: 10th IFIP/IEEE International Symposium on Integrated Network Management, IM 2007, pp. 469–477 (2007)
14. Takeuchi, S., Sezaki, K., Yasuda, Y.: Access point selection strategy in ieee802.11e wlan networks toward load balancing. Electronics and Communications in Japan (Part I: Communications) 90, 35–45 (2007)
15. Vasudevan, S., Papagiannaki, K., Diot, C., Kurose, J., Towsley, D.: Facilitating Access Point Selection in IEEE 802.11 Wireless Networks. In: Proceedings of the 5th ACM SIGCOMM Conference on Internet Measurement, IMC 2005, pp. 26–26. USENIX Association, Berkeley (2005)

Ph.D. Student Workshop — Management of Future Networking

SON Mechanism for Green Heterogeneous Cellular Networks

Luis Alejandro Fletscher [1,2(✉)], Catalina Valencia [1],
and Juan Felipe Botero[2]

[1]Processes and Energy School. Faculty of Mines, Universidad Nacional de Colombia,
Medellin, Colombia
{lafletscherb,cavalenciapa}@unal.edu.co
[2]Electronic and Telecommunications Department, Universidad de Antioquia,
Medellin, Colombia
{luis.fletscher,juanf.botero}@udea.edu.co

Abstract. Alternative energies are a good option to face the growing demand of energy consumption in the present and future telecommunications systems, particularly in the next generation cellular systems, where a significant increase in the number of nodes is expected. Although, there are still major challenges related to optimization of consumption in scenarios without grid connection, as well as the joint optimization of the radio resource and energy utilization.

A flexible architecture that allows to minimize the total energy consumption of the system is required, both for network design and power management, subject to variability of the alternative energy sources and operating restrictions of the cellular network, such as mobility parameters, coverage zone, load balancing and quality of service.

In this way, this project aims to propose a methodology for cellular phone network design in places without grid connection and a SON (Self Organized Networks) mechanism to dynamically control an energy-efficient system that includes renewable energy to power Heterogeneous Networks (HetNets), while optimizing the available radio resources.

Keywords: Energy efficiency · HetNets · SON · Green communications · Renewable energies · Optimal control

1 Introduction

The Green IT New Industry Shockwave published by Gartner [1] shows that the field of Information Technology and Communication (ICT) accounts for 2% of the CO_2 footprint. Similarly, within this field, mobile communications networks consume about 0.5% of global energy supply [2]. Therefore, the development of strategies to mitigate the environmental impact and improve energy consumption in future cellular networks is a field of research that is becoming paramount.

This work has been supported by the Doctoral Fellowships Program of COLCIENCIAS and CODI sustainability strategy 2014-2015 of the University of Antioquia.

© IFIP International Federation for Information Processing 2015
S. Latré et al. (Eds.): AIMS 2015, LNCS 9122, pp. 45–49, 2015.
DOI: 10.1007/978-3-319-20034-7_4

Among several strategies studied by manufacturers and academia to improve the energy efficiency in cellular networks, there are some related to the optimization of the consumption in network components or techniques to switch on-off different nodes [3, 4, 5, 6], but is not common to find an approach from the viewpoint of the energetic processes, i.e. on-place energy availability is an issue, even more relevant for isolated nodes [7].

In this way, a recent research topic is the integration of renewable energy (RE), such as wind and solar in places without connection to power grid. This opens research issues providing an important opportunity for both green cellular networks and facilitates the integration of REs in the infrastructure of the country [8, 9].

Similarly, another important research field is Self-Organizing Networks (SON) technology [10], which is able to minimize human intervention in the design and management of networking processes, counting now with architectures proposed for implementation in future cellular systems.

Therefore, this paper presents an overview of the doctoral project in Energy Systems whose main research goal is to propose a dynamic control algorithm and a methodology for network layout that provides energy efficient management in HetNets through a power system based in alternative energies, supported in a SON layer that adapts itself to improve the consumption to the current RE availability and to optimize the power radiated in areas without grid connection.

This paper is structured as follows: Section 2 presents the research problem, Section 3 describes the methodology approach. In Section 4, the foreseen impacts are presented, and finally the expected contribution and some conclusions are presented in Section 5.

2   Research Problem

Heterogeneous Networks or HetNets, are composed by coexisting macrocells and low power nodes (LPNs) such as picocells, femtocells, and relay nodes with the target of establishing a flexible architecture and respond to the growing traffic demand [11].

The deployment of a large number of LPNs carries on the ever increasing energy consumption in wireless networks, consumption that is today almost exclusively provided by the fossil originated or grid electricity, hindering the service in places without connection to the grid. In this context, the concept of Green Power Technology appears in the mobile industry, traditionally referring to a renewable energy source used to generate and supply power to a mobile base station site [12].

The implementation of renewable energy sources in cellular networks has several challenges. Some of them come from the unavailability of grid connection in many places plus the variability of the sun and wind energy. To solve these problems, control strategies are needed to balance both, energy sources consumption and management of the service, that is: accepting or transferring user connections from node to node, or reducing coverage area by sector or by emitted power. The implementation of the above mentioned control management strategies could also cause reduction in electromagnetic emissions and at the same time energy saving. Besides the need to modify dynamically the coverage area of the cell, structures a new and challenging research area.

In this sense, SON which is able to minimize human intervention in networking processes, combined with a dynamic optimization scheme to implement energy management control policies, offers a new perspective that has not been proposed yet in Green Cellular Networks research.

Thus, it is necessary to define a mechanism that combines the existing definition of SON with a dynamic optimization control system, such that it will be possible to perform an energy aware management of the network with a flexible and scalable scheme. To make this happen, the algorithms that optimize the operation of the alternative power supply and the communication protocols that coordinate the access to the network with the energy handling systems must be defined.

According to the above, we state that it is possible to generate a strategy that reduces the rate of global energy consumption in Heterogeneous Networks, by the implementation of an intelligent management system supported on alternative energy supply and by the implementation of a SON scheme that optimizes the use of radio resources that fulfills the requirements for quality of the service and properly manages the radiated power.

3   Research Objective and Methodology Approach

The objective of the project is to propose a dynamic control algorithm and a methodology for network layout that provides energy efficient management in HetNets through a power system based in alternative energies, supported in a SON layer that dynamically optimizes the radio resource utilization (coverages areas) and traffic management. In this sense, we propose an incremental methodology composed by the next steps:

1. Definition of an analytical model of alternative energy on-place availability and radio base consumption behavior: First step will be the Integration of the propagation model with the radio base consumption model [13] and the definition of the RE power availability based on geographical location of the base stations.
2. Static Optimization of the Network layout: Once the consumption model is defined, network layout could be defined by optimizing base stations location according to the availability of RE resource. This optimization is called "Static" in this work, because, quantity and location of base stations are defined prior to actual implementation of the cellular phone network.
3. Propose of a dynamic optimization mechanism: To optimize the utilization of green energy is necessary to formulate a model of the demand and consumption of energy by the different cells. This model should include the different parameters that affect the behavior of alternative energy sources, like traffic behavior, radio resources variation and weather forecasting to include them as constraints in the optimization process.

   The implementation of a SON based energy management system, will be used to optimize the consumption. This implementation will use renewable energy

sources according to its available power prediction through meteorological data and the power requested due to users of the area. This optimization is called "Dynamic" in this work, because a dynamic non-linear optimization will be performed by a controller each time step on each base station according to the technique described in [14].
4. Validation of the proposed architecture: Using weather forecast and traffic behavior data, simulation campaigns will be executed to test the proposed management optimization policies.

4   Foreseen Impact

The first impact of the project will be the formulation of an analytic model of energy consumption in heterogeneous networks including aspects related to quality of service and, from it, the implementation of a SON based energy management system to optimize the consumption using renewable energy sources.

In this way, the research project proposes to improve the energy efficiency and the reduction of CO_2 emissions with the design of a renewable energy system for cellular base stations. This will provide the opportunity to obtain greener communications and to integrate the renewable energy in the existing infrastructure at the same time.

Another important impact resulting of the Static optimization stage, will be a methodology for network design in places without grid connection.

According to the above, the main impact of this research will be to incorporate alternatives energies as a supplementary power source to traditional schemes and supporting the intelligence of the solution in an SON scheme, this way reducing the environmental impact of these technologies and guaranteeing the quality of service on isolated areas.

5   Conclusions

The use of alternative energy in telecommunication systems has been considered for decades, but there are still challenges to be overcome before its proper implementation in current systems. Within the fields of research that exist today, it is the development of control systems to establish load balancing between alternative energy sources and quality of service in places without grid connection.

One of the main current research topics is related to smart control systems, because the complexity of the new network architecture, the growing number of nodes and the presence of important variables as the traffic load, mobility and the radiated power, make optimization processes very complex, requiring therefore algorithms that are able to incorporate all these elements and generate feasible operation solutions.

For the proper application of renewable energy to HetNets, it is necessary to combine the strategy of supply with mechanisms to automatically organize the power levels that radiate each base station, to thereby minimize consumption fulfilling with the services requirements. Finally, is important say that one innovation factor of the doctoral proposal is the new approach to improve energy efficiency in HetNets.

References

1. Gartner: Green IT The New Industry Shockwave. In: Symposium/ITXPO Conference (2007)
2. Lubrittoa, C., Petragliaa, A., Vetromilea, C., Curcurutob, S., Logorellib, M., Marsicob, G., D'Onofrioa, A.: Energy and Environmental Aspects of Mobile Communication Systems. Energy 36, 1109–1114 (2011)
3. Auer, G., Giannini, V., Desset, C., Godor, I., Skillermark, P., Olsson, M., Imran, M.A., Sabella, D., Gonzalez, M.J., Blume, O., Fehske, A.: How much energy is needed to run a wireless network. IEEE Wireless Communications 18(5), 40–49 (2011)
4. Rao, J.B., Fapojuwo, A.O.: A Survey of Energy Efficient Resource Management Techniques for Multicell Cellular Networks. IEEE Communications Surveys & Tutorials 16(1), 154–180 (2014)
5. Navaratnarajah, S., Saeed, A., Dianati, M., Imran, M.A.: Energy Efficiency in Heterogeneous Wireless Access Networks. IEEE Wireless Communications 20(5), 37–43 (2013)
6. Yun, L., Celebi, H., Daneshmand, M., Chonggang, W., Weiliang, Z.: Energy-Efficient Femtocell Networks: Challenges and Opportunities. IEEE Wireless Communications 20(6), 99–105 (2013)
7. Morea, F., Viciguerra, G., Cucchi, D., Valencia, C.: Life Cycle Cost Evaluation of off-grid PV-wind Hybrid Power Systems. In: IEEE 29th International Telecommunications Energy Conference, INTELEC 2007, pp. 439–441. IEEE press, Rome (2007)
8. Han, T., Ansari, N.: Powering Mobile Networks with Green Energy. IEEE Wireless Communications 21(1), 90–96 (2014)
9. Al Haj Hassan, H., Nuaymi, L., Pelov, A.: Classification of Renewable Energy Scenarios and Objectives for Cellular Networks. In: IEEE 24th International Symposium on Personal, Indoor and Mobile Radio Communications: Mobile and Wireless Networks, pp. 2967 – 2972.IEEE press, London (2013)
10. Peng, M., Liang, D., Wei, Y., Li, J., Chen, H.: Self-Configuration and Self-Optimization in LTE-Advanced Heterogeneous Networks. IEEE Communications Magazine 51(5), 36–45 (2013)
11. Andrews, J.: Seven Ways that HetNets Are a Cellular Paradigm Shift. IEEE Communications Magazine 51(3), 136–144 (2013)
12. Hasan, Z., Boostanimehr, H., Bhargava, V.K.: Green Cellular Networks: A Survey, Some Research Issues and Challenges. IEEE Communications Surveys & Tutorials 13(4), 524–540 (2012)
13. Auer, G., Giannini, V., Desset, C., Godor, I., Skillermark, P., Olsson, M., Imran, M.A., Sabella, D., Gonzalez, M.J., Blume, O., Fehske, A.: How much energy is needed to run a wireless network? IEEE Wireless Communications 18(5), 40–49 (2011)
14. Valencia Peroni, C., Kasaire, N.S., Lee, J.H.: Optimal control of a fed-batch bioreactor using simulation-based approximate dynamic programming. IEEE Transactions on Control Systems Technology 13(5), 786–790 (2005)

QoE-Centric Management of Advanced Multimedia Services

Stefano Petrangeli[✉] and Filip De Turck

Department of Information Technology (INTEC), Ghent University–iMinds
Gaston Crommenlaan 8 (Bus 201), 9050 Ghent, Belgium
stefano.petrangeli@intec.ugent.be

Abstract. Over the last years, multimedia content has become more prominent than ever. Particularly, video streaming is responsible for more than a half of the total global bandwidth consumption on the Internet. As the original Internet was not designed to deliver such real-time, bandwidth-consuming applications, a serious challenge is posed on how to efficiently provide the best service to the users. This requires a shift in the classical approach used to deliver multimedia content, from a pure Quality of Service (QoS) to a full Quality of Experience (QoE) perspective. While QoS parameters are mainly related to low-level network aspects, the QoE reflects how the end-users perceive a particular multimedia service. As the relationship between QoS parameters and QoE is far from linear, a classical QoS-centric delivery is not able to fully optimize the quality as perceived by the users. This paper provides an overview of the main challenges this PhD aims to tackle in the field of end-to-end QoE optimization of video streaming services and, more precisely, of HTTP Adaptive Streaming (HAS) solutions, which are quickly becoming the de facto standard for video delivery over the Internet.

Keywords: Quality of Experience · Multimedia delivery · Multi-agent algorithms · Adaptive video streaming

1 Introduction

Nowadays, multimedia applications are responsible for an important portion of the traffic exchanged over the Internet. As an example, video streaming is responsible for more than a half of the total global bandwidth consumption on the Internet [1]. The continuous growth of these bandwidth-consuming and real-time applications poses a serious challenge on how to efficiently deliver multimedia content over the Internet. As an efficient delivery depends on the quality as perceived by the final user, the so-called Quality of Experience (QoE), a shift is required from a classical Quality of Service (QoS)- to a full QoE-centric delivery. In this perspective, networks and services should be managed in order to guarantee specific QoE levels instead of classical QoS parameters, which are unable to reflect the actual delivered QoE. A pure QoE-centric management is challenged by the nature of the Internet itself, as the Internet was not originally designed to support today's complex and high demanding services. In this PhD we investigate this challenging topic in detail and focus on the following research

© IFIP International Federation for Information Processing 2015
S. Latré et al. (Eds.): AIMS 2015, LNCS 9122, pp. 50–55, 2015.
DOI: 10.1007/978-3-319-20034-7_5

questions: (i) how cooperation can be envisioned between the network and the applications to increase the QoE? (ii) how applications' algorithms can be made adaptive to highly varying network conditions? (iii) how to guarantee fairness from a QoE perspective to applications competing for shared network resources?

2   QoE-Centric Delivery of Adaptive Video Streams

This PhD research covers the design of an architecture and algorithms for the efficient management of multimedia content. Particularly, we focus on the efficient delivery of HTTP Adaptive video Streaming (HAS).

2.1   Motivation

HAS techniques have become very popular due to their flexibility, and can therefore be considered as the de facto standard for video streaming services over the Internet. Recently, a standardized solution has been proposed by MPEG, called Dynamic Adaptive Streaming over HTTP (DASH). In HAS, each video is temporally segmented and stored in different quality levels. Rate adaptation heuristics, deployed at the video player, allow the most appropriate level to be dynamically requested, based on the current network conditions. Nevertheless, several inefficiencies have still to be solved in order to further improve users' QoE. As reported by Akshabi et al., current heuristics perform sub-optimally when sudden bandwidth drops occur, therefore leading to freezes in the video play-out, the main factor influencing users' QoE [2]. This issue is aggravated in case of live events, where the video player buffer has to be kept as small as possible in order to reduce the play-out delay between the user and the live signal. Moreover, current solutions have been shown to be underperforming in a multi-client scenario [3], [4], [5]. Concretely, this means that clients streaming video at the same time negatively influence each other as they compete for shared network resources. Fairness issues are not due to TCP dynamics, but mainly arise from the rate adaptation algorithms, as they decide on the actual rate to download [3]. In this PhD, we aim to solving the aforementioned problems arising in the delivery of HAS streams. Particularly, we focus on two complementary aspects: (i) novel client-based rate adaptation heuristics to improve users' QoE and (ii) network-based systems to efficiently deliver HAS streams.

2.2   Proposed Approach and Methodology

As introduced previously, a drawback of current HAS systems is their unmanaged nature. In a classical HAS system, no information exchange is envisioned between the clients and the network nodes. The goal of this PhD is to reverse this paradigm in order to fully optimize the delivery of HAS streams, i.e., provide a better QoE and improve fairness among competing clients. Particularly, we focus on multi-client scenarios, where multiple clients stream video at the same time. A fundamental aspect to consider in this setting is that the rate adaptation

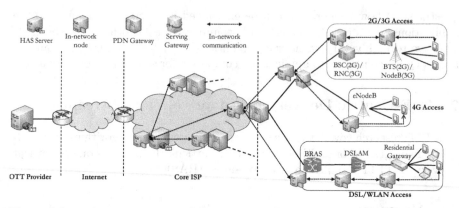

Fig. 1. Schematic representation of a communication network based on the Evolved Packet Core (EPC) [6]. The possible locations of the in-network nodes are shown. A node should be located at the main aggregation points of the network, in order to monitor the links where a bottleneck can occur.

heuristic of a client influences that of the other clients. When a client selects a particular quality level, it uses a portion of the shared bandwidth. This decision has an impact on the performance of the other clients and thus also on their rate adaptation. This means that a group of competing clients creates a *distributed control-feedback system*, whose performance is difficult to predict and influence.

In light of the above, the questions we aim to answering in this PhD are the following: (i) which feedback can be exchanged by the clients and the network nodes in order to have a fully cognitive delivery chain? (ii) which actions network nodes can take in order to help the clients achieving a high QoE and improving fairness? (iii) how can HAS clients proactively exploit the information provided by the network nodes to enhance the delivered QoE?

In order to tackle these questions, an in-network approach is investigated in this PhD. In this case, in-network nodes are placed in the network to collect feedback regarding the network and clients' conditions and influence client's behaviour. A possible positioning is shown in Figure 1. The main advantage of this approach is three-fold. First, no communication is needed among clients and consequently no significant overhead is introduced. Second, the quality level selection is still performed locally and independently by each client. Third, the approach is robust toward network failures, as the clients can also operate (at a sub-optimal level) without the in-network system. This problem can be modelled as a multi-agent system, where autonomous agents operate on local knowledge and posses only limited abilities, but they are nonetheless able to achieve a desired global behaviour (i.e., increase QoE and fairness). A first step in this area has been taken by us with the implementation of a rate adaptation heuristic based on a multi-agent version of the Q-Learning algorithm [5].

Obtained Results. Figure 2a shows some results from our proposal [5]. We investigate the performance of the proposed multi-client HAS framework, in comparison with both the Q-Learning-based client studied by Claeys et al. [7]

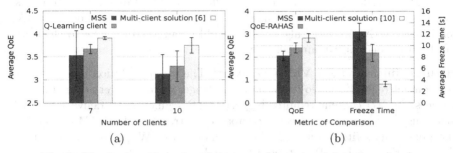

Fig. 2. Obtained results using the proposed in-network-based approach.

and a traditional HAS client, the Microsoft ISS Smooth Streaming (MSS) [8], in a scenario with 7 and 10 clients streaming video at the same time. Each bar represents the average QoE of the entire group of clients, together with its standard deviation that we use as fairness metric. The QoE is a metric in the same range of the Mean Opinion Score and can be computed as described by Claeys et al. [7]. In the evaluated bandwidth scenario, we were able to show that our multi-client HAS framework resulted in a better video quality and in a remarkable improvement of fairness, up to 60% and 48% in the 10 clients case, compared to MSS and the Q-Learning-based client, respectively. In Figure 2b, a comparison in terms of QoE and freeze time is provided with the MSS, the QoE-RAHAS heuristic [9] and our multi-client solution [10], in a scenario with 30 clients streaming video at the same time. By evaluating our solution under varying network conditions and in several multi-client scenarios, we showed how the proposed approach can reduce freezes up to 75% when compared to benchmark heuristics.

3   Conclusions and Future Work

This PhD aims to contributing to a more efficient delivery of multimedia content and, more specifically, of HTTP adaptive streams. We have proposed several new HAS heuristics able to dynamically adapt their behaviour depending on network conditions, in order to obtain a high QoE at the client. A fundamental element of our solution is a system of in-network nodes in charge of collecting information on the network and clients' conditions and improve clients' behaviour. Future research proceeds in three directions, which are detailed in the following.

Energy-Aware Management. Given the consumption of video from mobile devices is constantly increasing, rate adaptation heuristics should become aware and able to adapt to the characteristics of the mobile devices (e.g., CPU, battery lifetime). For this purpose, a MPEG–DASH compliant video player has been developed in order to test the proposed algorithms on real equipment [11].

Heterogeneous Clients. In real scenarios, different devices with different characteristics, e.g., in terms of screen dimension or subscription level, stream video together. The quality delivered to each device should be tailored based on these characteristics. This would also allow to introduce new business models in HAS services. How the proposed algorithms should be adapted in order to efficiently tackle this aspect is still an open topic.

High-Definition (HD) Video Delivery. The rapid evolution toward super-HD content (e.g., 4K video) poses new challenges in the delivery of multimedia services. As HD content requires bigger HTTP segments, its delivery is much more susceptible to video freezes compared to traditional one. Moreover, the effect of quality switches on QoE is further made worse. We propose to investigate the use of the new HTTP/2 standard to further increase the performance of the proposed algorithms in this scenario.

Acknowledgement. This work was partly funded by FLAMINGO, a Network of Excellence project (ICT–318488) supported by the European Commission under its Seventh Framework Programme.

References

1. Cisco Systems, Cisco Visual Networking Index: Forecast and Methodology, 2012–2017, http://www.cisco.com/c/en/us/solutions/collateral/service-provider/ip-ngn-ip-next-generation-network/white_paper_c11-481360.html (last visited March 2015)
2. Akhshabi, S., Narayanaswamy, S., Begen, A.C., Dovrolis, C.: An Experimental Evaluation of Rate-adaptive Video Players over HTTP. Signal Processing: Image Communication 27(4), 271–287 (2012)
3. Akhshabi, S., Anantakrishnan, L., Begen, A.C., Dovrolis, C.: What Happens when HTTP Adaptive Streaming Players Compete for Bandwidth? In: 22nd International Workshop on Network and Operating System Support for Digital Audio and Video (NOSSDAV 2012), pp. 9–14. ACM, Toronto (2012)
4. Li, Z., Zhu, X., Gahm, J., Pan, R., Hu, H., Begen, A.C., Oran, D.: Probe and Adapt: Rate Adaptation for HTTP Video Streaming At Scale. IEEE Journal on Selected Areas in Communications 32(4), 719–733 (2014)
5. Petrangeli, S., Claeys, M., Latré, S., Famaey, J., De Turck, F.: A Multi-agent Q-Learning-based Framework for Achieving Fairness in HTTP Adaptive Streaming. In: 2014 IEEE Network Operations and Management Symposium (NOMS), pp. 1–9. IEEE, Krakow, Poland (2014)
6. 3rd Generation Partnership Project (3GPP), 3GPP system - fixed broadband access network interworking (3GPP TS 23.139 version 11.3.0 Release 11), http://www.3gpp.org/DynaReport/23139.htm (last visited: March 2015)
7. Claeys, M., Latré, S., Famaey, J., Wu, T., Van Leekwijck, W., De Turck, F.: Design and Optimization of a (FA)Q-Learning-based HTTP Adaptive Streaming Client. Connection Science 26(01), 27–45 (2014)
8. Zambelli, A.: Microsoft ISS Smooth Streaming (MSS) client, https://slextensions.svn.codeplex.com/svn/trunk/SLExtensions/ AdaptiveStreaming (last visited: March 2015)
9. Petrangeli, S., Famaey, J., Claeys, M., De Turck, F.: A QoE-driven Rate Adaptation Heuristic for Enhanced Adaptive Video Streaming, http://users.ugent.be/spetrang/QoE-RAHAS.pdf (last visited: March 2015)

10. Petrangeli, S., Wauters, T., Huysegems, R., Bostoen, T., De Turck, F.: Network-based Dynamic Prioritization of HTTP Adaptive Streams to Avoid Video Freezes. In: 2015 IFIP/IEEE International Workshop on Quality of Experience Centric Management (QCMan), Ottawa, Canada (May 2015)
11. Petrangeli, S., Bouten, N., Dejonghe, E., Famaey, J., Leroux, P., De Turck, F.: Design and Evaluation of a DASH-compliant Second Screen Video Player for Live Events in Mobile Scenarios. In: 2015 IEEE/IFIP International Symposium on Integrated Network Management (IM), Ottawa, Canada (May 2015)

Exploring IoT Protocols Through
the Information-Centric Networking's Lens

Salvatore Signorello[1(✉)], Radu State[1], and Olivier Festor[2]

[1] SnT, University of Luxembourg, Luxembourg, Luxembourg
{salvatore.signorello,radu.state}@uni.lu
[2] Inria Nancy-Grand Est, Villers-les-Nancy, France
olivier.festor@inria.fr

Abstract. Information-Centric Networking (ICN) advocates a clean-slate redesign of the Internet network layer through a major shift from a host-to-host communication model to a content-based one. Hence ideally, current ICN propositions and implementations, for instance NDN (Named Data Networking), should replace the IP layer. Indeed none of these already provide a full-fledged solution, due to the big challenges that their deployment at a global scale implies. Nevertheless ICN's ambitious goal could be a plausible short-term step for networks at the Internet's borders, where several layer-2 technologies populate the Internet of Things ecosystem. Those domains still need an in-depth analysis of the potential of the ICN solutions as well as of the concrete mechanisms to deploy them. Thus in the following, we've sketched out our research path to find out common layer-2 requirements for the future Internet's network-layer.

Keywords: ICN · Network-layer · NDN · IoT

1 Introduction

The Internet's architecture has notably served our needs so far, even if, since its original design, the requirements for a global communication infrastructure have radically changed [1]. Nowadays many researchers finally have agreed on the concrete need for a redesign of the network architecture to improve its efficiency and to assure it a longer life. A novel networking approach, called Information-Centric Networking [2], suggests to shift the model of communication used by the Internet from a host-to-host dialogue to a network-driven search for sources of information.

Since the coming out of PARC with Van Jacobson's google-talk [15] and the subsequent publication of the seminal paper on Content-Centric Networking [4] have spread the idea of Information Centric Networking, several advances have been done in the field. As counterpart, there are still several critical research challenges [16] that need to be addressed by ICN and those unanswered questions slow down its adoption.

© IFIP International Federation for Information Processing 2015
S. Latré et al. (Eds.): AIMS 2015, LNCS 9122, pp. 56–60, 2015.
DOI: 10.1007/978-3-319-20034-7_6

Today the ICN community eagerly seeks use-cases to showcase the advantages this novel network paradigm might bring in real-life scenarios [18]. To this regard, the ICN data-oriented approach appeals to the Internet of Things (IoT) domain as the perfect glue for internetworking the IoT islands. Nevertheless previous research works have just showcased the feasibility of adopting ICN for some specific IoT scenarios, e.g., BASs [5,6], MANETs [7,8], vehicular networks [9,10] and sink-centric WSNs [11,12,13]. Each of those attempts relies on ad-hoc assumptions and none of them identify a common set of services that an ICN layer should expose to the IoT's layer-2 technologies. This lack of consensus on few core design principles implies that current ICN solutions often have to be heavily tailored for the deployment in IoT scenarios.

2   Background on Named Data Networking

The NDN architecture [3] is the ICN instantiation targeted for our study. The NDN communication model is receiver-driven and it is governed by two different named network packets, the *Interest* and the *Data*, and by three data structures, the Forwarding Information Base (FIB), the Pending Interest Table (PIT) and the Content Store (CS). The communication is started by information consumers that issue *Interests* to request contents. Then the network routes by name the *Interests* (matching FIB entries held by the network devices) towards one or more content providers (either the original source or devices that have cached a copy in their CS). Finally the Data is routed back to the requester, following the trail left (the PIT entries) by the corresponding Interest into the traversed network devices.

NDN features several design choices that appeal to the IoT. It provides in-network caching and content-based security (every packet carries a digital signature) that might reduce the duty cycle of constrained-resources devices, as long as the information they've disseminated will be valid. It provides flow balance mechanisms, matching an *Interest* to a single *Data* packet, that might reduce the overall traffic and so the demand for computation into the network devices. It allows to define human-readable naming schemes to address the network's contents, and this might ease the services and objects discovery which is crucial in IoT dense environments. Moreover NDN performs multi-path name-based forwarding of network packets, that is, a network device can forward a request to multiple next hops based both on some information it holds and on the request's name. The forwarding logic can be further specialized through the plug-in of user-defined software modules, called strategies, to perform custom forwarding decisions.

3   Research Statement

The Internet was originally devised to deliver packets to fixed destination addresses and now it is expected to serve billions of mobile devices jumping between different networks. Any clean-slate attempt to evolve the Internet's architecture has to accommodate both emerging and consolidated technologies in a fresh design. So any conscious advocate of ICN should ask himself: "Is ICN ready to welcome the Internet-of-Things?"

The success of the Internet Protocol stems from the neat layered design of the whole network architecture. At the Internet's rise the main requirements for a global network were translated into IP's packet format fields. For instance, the need of internetworking was barely encoded into the IP datagram format as fragmentation fields and, not surprisingly, it is still of immense relevance. The history of computer networks has taught us that there will always be layer-2 technologies with different requirements that need to inter-operate and this aspect has become more and more evident with the proliferation of network technologies throughout the last decade: WiFi, WiMAX, Bluetooth, LoWPANs standards, 4G and sooner its descendant 5G.

ICN has potential features to welcome the heterogeneity of technologies that characterizes the IoT, but it has evidently not been designed to fulfill this objective. Therefore, we strive to enhance the design of current ICN solutions through the analysis of their deployment in scenarios where end-users join several networks at the same time. In figure 1 we illustrate one of the scenarios on target. We suppose to have an user with a laptop equipped with three different network interfaces. The user's laptop has an Ethernet interface plugged to a private company LAN. At the same time the user has joined a different ad-hoc WiFi network with some colleagues to do collaborative tasks. Finally, the user also has broadband Internet access, e.g., through either an usb-modem for cellular connection or PC-card for WiMAX access.

Fig. 1. Targeted use case scenario

One trivial use-case for the scenario depicted above could be the following: the user wants to fetch some content from the web and some of his colleagues might have already fetched the same; so if some local copies exist, the user would prefer to fetch them for many possible reasons, e.g., to save traffic, to have faster download times, to not worry about cellular connection instability. Each time the user's application make a call to a network primitive, the network level should try to fit out the best from the local resources and from the neighborhood. So the question is: "Are current ICN solutions really ready to serve to this need?"

4   Methodology and Preliminary Results

Our research roadmap mainly targets the testing and the extension of the NDN's platform codebase [19]. However we use in parallel the network simulator ndnSim [14] based on the ns-3, a network simulator that offers modules modeling the most common layer-2 technologies.

We've tested how the plain NDN performs in simple scenarios wherein some nodes exhibit both WiFi and Ethernet connectivity. We've run some rounds of simulation over a three-level tree network topology, where all the leaf nodes fetch content from a single producer at the root of the tree, see figure 2. We've run the experiments for three distinct scenarios, namely labeled as *Caching*, *WiFi*, *WiFi & Caching*. In the *Caching* scenario, all the tree nodes cache content, but none of them have WiFi connectivity. In the *WiFi* scenario, leaf nodes have WiFi and they're the only tree nodes that can cache contents. In the *WiFi &* *Caching* scenario, leaf nodes have WiFi and all the tree nodes can cache content. In fig. 3 we've reported the average download time measured using different built-in ndnSim's forwarding strategies [17]. Surprisingly the average download time never decreases in presence of cached contents by the consumer's WiFi-neighbors, on the contrary it worsens. The latter condition happens because of the high collision rate produced by the intense broadcast WiFi traffic [20].

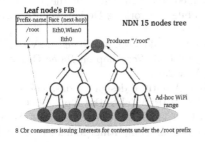

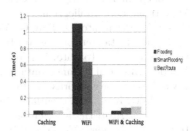

Fig. 2. Topology for preliminary tests   **Fig. 3.** Average download time

5   Conclusion

As expected, this first hands-on experience outlines that the NDN protocol, as it is, cannot run efficiently over different layer-2 without adaptation and thus it calls for a deeper investigation. As next step, we've started implementing a custom forwarding strategy into ndnSim, which prioritizes output interfaces according to their data-link layer.

References

1. Braden, R., Clark, D., Shenker, S., Wroclawski, J.: Developing a Next-Generation Internet Architecture. White paper, DARPA (July 2000)
2. Ahlgren, B., Dannewitz, C., Imbrenda, C., Kutscher, D., Ohlman, B.: A survey of Information-Centric Networking. IEEE Communications 50(7), 26–36 (2012)
3. Zhang, L., Afanasyev, A., Burke, J., Jacobson, V., Claffy, K., Crowley, P., Papadopoulos, C., Wang, L., Zhang, B.: Named Data Networking. ACM SIGCOMM Computer Communication Review (CCR) (July 2014)
4. Jacobson, V., Smetters, D.K., Thornton, J.D., Plass, M.F., Briggs, N.H., Braynard, R.L.: Networking named content. In: International Conference on Emerging Networking Experiments and Technologies, CoNEXT. ACM (2009)
5. Burke, J., Gasti, P., Nathan, N., Tsudik, G.: Securing Instrumented Environments over Content-Centric Networking: the Case of Lighting Control and NDN. In: IEEE INFOCOM NOMEN Workshop (2013)
6. Zhang, J., Li, Q., Schooler, E.M.: iHEMS an Information-Centric approach to secure home energy management. In: IEEE SmartGridComm (2012)
7. Yu, Y., et al.: Interest propagation in named data manets. In: Proc. of IEEE ICNC, pp. 1118–1122 (2013)
8. Meisel, M., Pappas, V., Zhang, L.: Ad Hoc Networking via Named Data. ACM MobiArch (2010)
9. Wang, L., Afanasyev, A., Kuntz, R., Vuyyuru, R., Wakikawa, R., Zhang, L.: Rapid traffic information dissemination using named data. In: Proc. of the 1st ACM Workshop on Emerging Name-Oriented Mobile Networking Design-Architecture, Algorithms, and Applications, pp. 7–12. ACM (2012)
10. Grassi, G., Pasavento, D., Pau, G., Vuyyuru, R., Wakikawa, R., Zhang, L.: VANET via Named Data Networking. In: IEEE INFOCOM Workshop on Name Oriented Mobility (NOM), Toronto, Canada (April-May 2014)
11. Amadeo, M., et al.: Named data networking: A natural design for data collection in wireless sensor networks. In: Proc. of IEEE/IFIP Wireless Days, pp. 1–6 (2013)
12. Dinh, N.-T., Kim, Y.: Potential of Information-Centric Wireless Sensor and Actor Networking. In: IEEE International Conference on Computing, Management and Telecommunications (ComManTel) (2013)
13. Francois, J., Cholez, T., Engel, T.: CCN Traffic Optimization for IoT. In: The 4th International Conf. on Network of the Future (NoF) (2013)
14. Afanasyev, A., Moiseenko, I., Zhang, L.: ndnSIM: NDN simulator for NS-3. NDN Technical Report NDN-0005 (revision October 2, 2012)
15. Jacobson, V.: A new way to look at networking. Google Tech Talk, https://www.youtube.com/watch?v=oCZMoY3q2uM
16. ICN Research Challenges draft-kutscher-icnrg-challenges-02, http://datatracker.ietf.org/doc/draft-kutscher-icnrg-challenges/
17. ndnSim's Forwarding Strategies, http://ndnsim.net/1.0/fw.html
18. Information-Centric Networking: Baseline Scenarios draft-irtf-icnrg-scenarios-03, https://datatracker.ietf.org/doc/draft-irtf-icnrg-scenarios/
19. The named-data networking project's website, http://named-data.net/
20. Campolo, C., Molinaro, A., Casetti, C., Chiasserini, C.-F.: An 802.11-based MAC Protocol for Reliable Multicast in Multihop Networks. In: Proc. of Vehicular Technology Conference, pp. 1–5 (April 2009)

Towards a Fluid Cloud: An Extension of the Cloud into the Local Network

Bart Spinnewyn[✉] and Steven Latré

Department of Mathematics and Computer Science, University of Antwerp - iMinds,
Middelheimlaan 1, 2020, Antwerp, Belgium
bart.spinnewyn@uantwerpen.be

Abstract. Cloud computing offers an attractive platform to provide resources on-demand, but currently fails to meet the corresponding latency
requirements for a wide range of Internet of Things (IoT) applications. In
recent years efforts have been made to distribute the cloud closer to the
user environment, but they were typically limited to the fixed network
infrastructure as current cloud management algorithms cannot cope with
the unpredictable nature of wireless networks. This fixed deployment of
clouds often does not suffice as, for some applications, the access network
itself already introduces an intolerable delay in response time. Therefore
we propose to extend the cloud formalism into the (wireless) IoT environment itself, incorporating the infrastructure that is already present.
Given the mobile nature of local infrastructure, we refer to this as a fluid
extension to the cloud, or more simply as a fluid cloud.

1 Introduction

While the Internet was originally intended as a dumb packet forwarder between
fixed (large) computers, it now comprises a myriad of devices connected through
a plethora of technologies and used for a wide range of applications. This unexpected evolution has fuelled the popularity and reach of the current Internet but
has also put a significant strain on its management complexity. During recent
years, two major trends have presented themselves that will define the Internet's
management for the next decades: cloud computing and the Internet of Things.
Cloud computing is enabled by large-scale datacentres hosting hundreds of thousands of servers, offering resources on a pay-per-use basis. The management
of fixed cloud infrastructure has already extensively been studied in literature.
Moens et al. propose a feature model, incorporating interdependencies between
application features [1]. Zhani et al. advocate Virtual Datacentre Embedding
(VDE) as a means of guaranteeing both server and network resources [2]. This
is closely related to the work on Virtual Network Embedding (VNE) [3], [4], [5].
Here, virtual network components are embedded into a physical network substrate, similar to how virtual machines are embedded into a physical machine
substrate. Another trend in the management of cloud computing is the inter-
cloud paradigm, where not one cloud is considered but researchers focus on the
optimal distribution of computational tasks between multiple clouds [6]. This

© IFIP International Federation for Information Processing 2015
S. Latré et al. (Eds.): AIMS 2015, LNCS 9122, pp. 61–65, 2015.
DOI: 10.1007/978-3-319-20034-7_7

network of clouds is needed to ensure that some tasks are deployed on an infrastructure that is closer to the user. In more complex environments, a complete collection of private clouds is considered. Latency and jitter are becoming the dominant concerns in the application placement problem as they are typically used for applications that require a rapid response [7]. Nearby clouds generally perform better in terms of latency. This consideration eventually leads to the conception of fog computing. Urgaonkar et al. define the fog as a cloud close to the ground [7]. They propose placement of computational entities at the Internet Service Provider (ISP) level to lower latency and jitter.

A second important trend in communication networks is the recent emergence of the Internet of Things (IoT) paradigm. The developments in wireless technology and the price drop for miniaturized electronic components have fuelled the uptake of connected objects. Early products are in the meantime present in all market segments, and range from our personal devices and appliances over public infrastructures to industrial machinery. Future highly interactive applications will require ultra-low response times, these applications include robotics [8] and human-machine interactions [9]. Rapid growth of connected devices introduces new challenges e.g. with respect to ubiquitous wireless connectivity, efficient allocation of networking and computing resources, the real-time processing of continuous IoT data streams and the novel types of interactions that may emerge between humans and their smart, connected environment [10].

As a single sensor node typically does not have appropriate computational capabilities, tasks in an IoT environment are currently offloaded to a nearby server. While concepts such as cloud computing allow delegating these tasks to a computational infrastructure, it may not always be possible to use this centralized infrastructure e.g. because the introduced latency between the wireless link and fixed infrastructure is too high. Concepts such as the inter-cloud and fog computing are thus a first step towards solving this latency challenge but they are not able to support the required really fast response times for highly interactive applications.

2   Fluid Cloud

This paper proposes to extend the cloud formalism into the (wireless) IoT environment itself, incorporating the infrastructure that is already present and can be accessed at minimal latency. Given the mobile nature of the local infrastructure, we will refer to this as a fluid extension to the cloud, or more simply as a fluid cloud. This extension however is non-trivial as local infrastructure drastically differs from traditional cloud infrastructure. State-of-the-art management concepts assume infrastructure to be static, always-on, highly performing in terms of memory and CPU, and interconnected by an over-provisioned, well-controlled network. These assumptions clearly are no longer valid in the context of an IoT environment. Fluid cloud management must consider a broad spectrum, which includes devices that are low-power, unreliable and constrained in terms of connectivity, memory and processing. In the following we describe how we plan

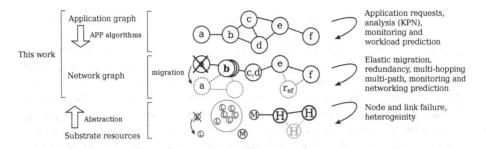

Fig. 1. Illustration of fluid cloud concepts: Processes c, d are consolidated onto one physical node, b is replicated onto multiple physical nodes. r_{ef} is a relay process that enables multi-hopping. A, b, c, d and c, d, e, f communicate over respectively wireless and wired infrastructure. Physical devices are non-restrictively labelled as either Low (L), Medium (M) or High (H) performance.

to overcome the challenges associated with extension of the cloud into an IoT environment. A high-level overview of the research project is given in Figure 1.

In a first phase, we will develop an IoT-aware application placement framework that handles requests for computational tasks and distributes these requests to available IoT infrastructure. Both initial and additional requests must be handled and the often dynamic QoS (Quality of Service) evolution in an IoT environment must be taken into account. Maximisation of the number of applications that can be hosted on the platform while satisfying resource limitations is referred to as the Application Placement Problem (APP), which in its general form is NP-hard [7], [11]. Efficient placement requires knowledge about the composition of applications. Therefore we will first develop a theoretical framework to describe applications as composed of processes, communicating over channels. We prefer a description in terms of processes as it allows use of elegant models such as Kahn Processing Networks (KPN) [12] and its extensions [13].

Secondly, we will use this theoretical framework for building new IoT-aware placement algorithms. Traditional application placement considers a list of machines, each having limited CPU and memory resources available and a list containing application processes, each having a certain demand for said resources. Limitations on machine resources, such as CPU and memory, will be incorporated as Knapsack constraints. Recent works incorporate bandwidth limitations as a third resource type. However such an approach implicitly assumes the networking interfaces of individual machines bottleneck throughput. This assumption is clearly not valid in an IoT environment, as the networking infrastructure cannot be assumed reliable and over-provisioned. Therefore, we will add topology-awareness to both application and networking description. In this context, we will extend the theoretical framework by translating application specifications into an application graph, displaying task-level parallelism and dependencies. Moreover, a network graph will be generated, representing Knapsack and QoS constraints as vertices and edges respectively. The network graph can be generated by instantiating monitoring components throughout the network.

Thirdly, traditional placement algorithms are said to be *binary*, indicating that a process is either placed once, or not at all. In an IoT environment, hosts are unreliable, as they can enter and leave the network at any time. We will mitigate this unreliable nature of hosts by grouped replication of processes. Individual processes can be placed multiple times, implicating that in our case the APP will be *non-binary*. Networking links can be highly unreliable. Therefore, on the other hand we will instantiate additional relay processes, enabling multi-hopping, a technique widely deployed in wireless mesh networks. This way placement algorithms gain control over routing, introducing an additional variable in QoS optimisation. Also we note that in QoS constrained applications, reliability of pair-wise communication between processes can be augmented by employing multiple parallel connections, referred to as multi-path routing.

In a second phase we will develop elastic migration algorithms to support migration of processes in live systems. Migration is called for when either networking environment or workload are altered significantly. In a QoS constrained system, migration tends to result in unacceptable delays, as this is a bandwidth and memory intensive procedure. Therefore, we will incorporate predictions to estimate future workload and networking conditions. Also, in our framework we will define multiple levels of QoS guarantees, each corresponding to certain networking conditions. As such we can define techniques of graceful degradation to cope with faults through system reconfiguration at runtime, at the cost of redundant active or standby resources. In this light, one needs to ensure the correct tasks restart after a system reconfiguration. Therefore, we will implement check-pointing protocols to support state reservation.

Acknowledgments. Part of this work has been funded by the iFEST and EMD project, co-funded by iMinds and IWT.

References

1. Moens, H., Truyen, E., Walraven, S., Joosen, W., Dhoedt, B., De Turck, F.: Feature placement algorithms for high-variability applications in cloud environments. In: 2012 IEEE Network Operations and Management Symposium (NOMS), pp. 17–24. IEEE (2012)
2. Zhani, M.F., Zhang, Q., Simon, G., Boutaba, R.: VDC planner: Dynamic migration-aware virtual data center embedding for clouds. In: 2013 IFIP/IEEE International Symposium on Integrated Network Management (IM 2013), pp. 18–25 (2013)
3. Fischer, A., Botero, J.F., Till Beck, M., De Meer, H., Hesselbach, X.: Virtual network embedding: A survey. IEEE Communications Surveys & Tutorials 15(4), 1888–1906 (2013)
4. Mijumbi, R., Gorricho, J.-L., Serrat, J., Claeys, M., Turck, F.D., Latré, S.: Design and evaluation of learning algorithms for dynamic resource management in virtual networks. In: 2014 IEEE Network Operations and Management Symposium (NOMS), pp. 1–9. IEEE (2014)

 5. Latre, S., Famaey, J., De Turck, F., Demeester, P.: The fluid internet: service-centric management of a virtualized future internet. IEEE Communications Magazine 52(1), 140–148 (2014)
 6. Buyya, R., Ranjan, R., Calheiros, R.N.: InterCloud: Utility-oriented federation of cloud computing environments for scaling of application services. In: Hsu, C.-H., Yang, L.T., Park, J.H., Yeo, S.-S. (eds.) ICA3PP 2010, Part I. LNCS, vol. 6081, pp. 13–31. Springer, Heidelberg (2010)
 7. Urgaonkar, B., Rosenberg, A.L., Shenoy, P.: Application placement on a cluster of servers. International Journal of Foundations of Computer Science 18(05), 1023–1041 (2007)
 8. Hu, G., Tay, W.P., Wen, Y.: Cloud robotics: architecture, challenges and applications. IEEE Network 26(3), 21–28 (2012)
 9. Wang, A.L., Canedo: Offloading industrial human-machine interaction tasks to mobile devices and the cloud. In: 2014 IEEE Emerging Technology and Factory Automation (ETFA), pp. 1–4 (September 2014)
10. Essa, I.A.: Ubiquitous sensing for smart and aware environments. IEEE Personal Communications 7(5), 47–49 (2000)
11. Camati, R.S., Calsavara, A., Lima Jr., L.: Solving the virtual machine placement problem as a multiple multidimensional knapsack problem. In: The Thirteenth International Conference on Networks, ICN 2014, pp. 253–260 (2014)
12. Vrba, Z., Halvorsen, C., Beskow, P.: Kahn process networks are a flexible alternative to MapReduce. In: 11th IEEE International Conference on High Performance Computing and Communications, HPCC 2009, pp. 154–162. IEEE (2009)
13. Copil, G., Moldovan, D., Truong, H.-L., Dustdar, S.: Sybl: An extensible language for controlling elasticity in cloud applications. In: 2013 13th IEEE/ACM International Symposium on Cluster, Cloud and Grid Computing (CCGrid), pp. 112–119 (May 2013)

Measuring and Modeling Multipath TCP

Viet-Hoang Tran$^{(\boxtimes)}$, Ramin Sadre, and Olivier Bonaventure

ICTEAM, Université catholique de Louvain, Louvain-la-Neuve, Belgium
{tranviet,ramin.sadre,olivier.bonaventure}@uclouvain.be

Abstract. Multipath TCP, a major extension to regular TCP, allows TCP clients to utilize multiple paths to improve the transfer rate and connection robustness. Providing these benefits without requiring to upgrade network infrastructure nor applications, Multipath TCP is becoming more popular. Notably Apple iOS 7 now supports it for SIRI. However, there is still lack of a complete understanding of Multipath TCP in practice. How much can a user benefit from Multipath TCP in different scenarios? Which factors affect the performance of Multipath TCP? How well can we predict the behavior of Multipath TCP in a specific environment? Our research aims to answer these questions by large-scale measurements and model-based analysis. The answers will be an important input for designers and developers to further improve Multipath TCP.

Keywords: Multipath · MPTCP · Traffic measurement · Modeling

1 Background

To be able to use several network paths for a single connection is a long-desired feature, since it would bring several benefits including higher transfer rate and better robustness. However, this is not possible with TCP – the dominating reliable protocol in today's Internet. As an extension for TCP, Multipath TCP (MPTCP) is rapidly adopted by both academia and industry. At the time of writing, MPTCP implementations exist on several operating systems, including Linux [10], Apple iOS and MacOS [1], FreeBSD [14], Solaris [5] and Citrix. A notable use case of MPTCP is to enable WiFi/3G offload on mobile devices [11,3,4]. On recent iPhones and iPads, Apple has deployed and enabled MPTCP by default for its voice recognition application (SIRI) [1] in order to reduce end-to-end delays. It could also be used in datacenters to exploit multiple paths between hosts [13]. Before MPTCP, Stream Control Transmission Protocol (SCTP) [6] was designed with multi-homing in mind and supports concurrent multipath extensions [9]. However, SCTP is still not widely used since it requires developers to change their applications and many networking devices like NATs/Firewalls do not understand SCTP and block its traffic. Instead, Multipath TCP was designed with backward-compatible goals in mind: it provides network applications the same API as regular TCP, for that TCP applications can use MPTCP without any modification. Behind the scene, it uses several subflows which appear to network infrastructure as separated regular TCP connections. Detailed explanations of MPTCP can be found in [7].

© IFIP International Federation for Information Processing 2015
S. Latré et al. (Eds.): AIMS 2015, LNCS 9122, pp. 66–70, 2015.
DOI: 10.1007/978-3-319-20034-7_8

2   Motivation and Research Problems

Given the quick adoption and the potential applications of MPTCP, it is important to know how reliable MPTCP is and how much performance we can gain from using it in practice. A thorough understanding of MPTCP behavior and performance now becomes critical. We have identified three major questions that need to be answered:

1. *How is MPTCP currently used?*
   In MPTCP, so-called *schedulers* and *path managers* control how subflows are established and how packets are distributed over them. Different implementations for scheduling and path managing are available. In order to further develop MPTCP, the designers of MPTCP need to know what users are currently using. Which configurations are used in practice? Can we find that from passive measurements? For what applications is MPTCP used?
2. *How does MPTCP behave in practice?*
   This can be split into more specific questions: whether MPTCP always behaves correctly, and how well the performance of MPTCP is. SCTP has been implemented in many operating systems, but its usage is very limited since it is incompatible with conventional TCP. Learned from the painfully slow adoption/deployment of SCTP, MPTCP was designed to work with conventional applications and network infrastructure. For example, MPTCP should fall back to regular TCP when proper operation over multiple paths is not possible. Until now, there is little knowledge about the correct behavior of MPTCP in such situations over the global Internet. In terms of performance, the fact that MPTCP uses several paths does not mean it will automatically gain the sum of goodput over all paths. Moreover, the perceived delay to the user is also important to investigate.
3. *How to predict the behavior of MPTCP before deploying it in a specific environment?*
   While MPTCP has potential to bring several benefits to a wide range of devices, network operators or service providers need to anticipate the benefits and the risks from deploying MPTCP on a large scale.

Generally, in order to answer the above questions, we can evaluate MPTCP through analysis, simulation, emulation [12], or real-world measurement. There are several existing efforts. Passive measurement is done by collecting the available information from the network, for example in [8], while active measurement is done by sending particular packets through networks and getting the necessary metrics [3,4]. There are also works toward modeling and analysis. For example, Arzani et al. [2] present a simple model for MPTCP behavior for a simple 2-path topology. However, to predict MPTCP behavior in a real, heterogeneous environment is still a big challenge.

3   Research Directions

We plan to answer research questions 1 and 2 by performing measurements. A first step was done in [8] where we collected and analyzed the MPTCP network

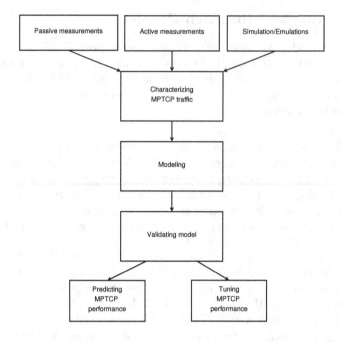

Fig. 1. Our methodology

traffic on a public Internet server for one week. This server hosts *multipath-tcp.org* site to which everyone interested in MPTCP can access, download kernel and do testing with MPTCP enabled. In order to gain a more general insight into the usage and behavior of MPTCP in practice, we need to conduct measurements with the following considerations in mind:

1. Large-scale measurement: Previous works, which mostly focused on active measurement, only tested MPTCP with a few hosts. We envisage to perform active and passive measurements on a large number and wide variety of hosts. Our current measurement [8] on *multipath-tcp.org* have users accessed from around the world, using a single or multiple network interfaces. Since the popularity of MPTCP is increasing, we have now for the first time the opportunity to observe MPTCP's behavior at large scale.
2. Dealing with a wide variety of MPTCP implementations: We want to develop techniques to identify the specific MPTCP implementation used by a host by passive measurements. This identification is an essential step in determining whether a particular observed behavior is due to the MPTCP protocol or due to a specific implementation.
3. Avoiding bias: Until recently, MPTCP was mainly used by people interested in this new technology. In order to avoid such kind of bias (and others, such as on the used operating system) in our measurements, we need to analyze passive measurement results to know more about the users of MPTCP.

To answer research question 3, we plan to build models of MPTCP behavior that can be applied to different network and host configurations. A first step could be to extend the work in [2] to more complex topologies and other schedulers. We expect that a general model will be hard to achieve. Instead, we will use the outcomes of our measurement activities to define and parametrize the most typical or interesting usage scenarios.

4   Conclusion

This paper presents the need for a thorough research of MPTCP behavior and usage in practice, and gives an overview on the challenges and directions of our research. We believe our work will bring a more comprehensive understanding of MPTCP protocol, implementations and traffic. This knowledge will be a valuable input for MPTCP designer to further improve the protocol. For the users, the work will give a more clear view on the benefit of using MPTCP and foster the widespread of MPTCP usage in practice.

Acknowledgments. This work has been carried out in the context of the METRICS project - an Initial Training Network (ITN) which is supported by the European Commission.

References

1. Apple. iOS: Multipath TCP Support in iOS 7., http://support.apple.com/en-us/HT201373
2. Arzani, B., Gurney, A., Cheng, S., Guerin, R., Thau Loo, B.: Deconstructing MPTCP Performance. In: 2014 IEEE 22nd International Conference on Network Protocols (ICNP), pp. 269–274 (October 2014)
3. Chen, Y.-C., Lim, Y.-S., Gibbens, R., Nahum, E., Khalili, R., Towsley, D.: A Measurement-based Study of Multipath TCP Performance over Wireless Networks. In: ACM SIGCOMM IMC (2013)
4. Deng, S., Netravali, R., Sivaraman, A., Balakrishnan, H.: WiFi, LTE, or Both?: Measuring Multi-Homed Wireless Internet Performance. In: Proceedings of the 2014 Conference on Internet Measurement Conference, IMC 2014, pp. 181–194. ACM, New York (2014)
5. Eardley, P.: Survey of MPTCP Implementations. Internet-Draft draft-eardley-mptcp-implementations-survey-02, IETF Secretariat (July 2013)
6. Stewart, R. (ed.): Stream Control Transmission Protocol. IETF RFC 4960 (September 2007)
7. Ford, A., Raiciu, C., Handley, M., Bonaventure, O.: TCP Extensions for Multipath Operation with Multiple Addresses. IETF RFC 6824 (January 2013)
8. Hesmans, B., Tran-Viet, H., Sadre, R., Bonaventure, B.: A First Look at Real Multipath TCP Traffic. In: 7th International Workshop on Traffic Monitoring and Analysis (TMA) (2015)
9. Iyengar, J., Amer, P., Stewart, R.: Concurrent Multipath Transfer Using SCTP Multihoming over Independent End-to-end Paths. IEEE/ACM Transactions on Networking 14(5), 951–964 (2006)

10. Paasch, C., Barre, S., et al.: Multipath TCP implementation in the Linux kernel (2014), http://www.multipath-tcp.org
11. Paasch, C., Detal, G., Duchene, F., Raiciu, C., Bonaventure, O.: Exploring Mobile/WiFi Handover with Multipath TCP. In: ACM SIGCOMM Workshop CellNet, pp. 31–36 (2012)
12. Paasch, C., Khalili, R., Bonaventure, O.: On the Benefits of Applying Experimental Design to Improve Multipath TCP. In: Proceedings of the Ninth ACM Conference on Emerging Networking Experiments and Technologies, CoNEXT 2013, pp. 393–398. ACM, New York (2013)
13. Raiciu, C., Barre, S., Pluntke, C., Greenhalgh, A., Wischik, D., Handley, M.: Improving Datacenter Performance and Robustness with Multipath TCP. In: ACM SIGCOMM 2011 (2011)
14. Williams, N., Stewart, L., Armitage, G.: FreeBSD kernel patch for Multipath TCP (July 2014), http://caia.swin.edu.au/urp/newtcp/mptcp/tools.html

Security, Privacy, and Measurements

Learning to Detect Network Intrusion from a Few Labeled Events and Background Traffic

Gustav Šourek[1]([⊠]), Ondřej Kuželka[2], and Filip Železný[1]

[1] CTU Prague, Prague, Czech Republic
{souregus,zelezny}@fel.cvut.cz
[2] Cardiff University, Cardiff, UK
kuzelkao@cardiff.ac.uk

Abstract. Intrusion detection systems (IDS) analyse network traffic data with the goal to reveal malicious activities and incidents. A general problem with learning within this domain is a lack of relevant ground truth data, i.e. real attacks, capturing malicious behaviors in their full variety. Most of existing solutions thus, up to a certain level, rely on rules designed by network domain experts. Although there are advantages to the use of rules, they lack the basic ability of adapting to traffic data. As a result, we propose an ensemble tree bagging classifier, capable of learning from an extremely small number of true attack representatives, and demonstrate that, incorporating a general background traffic, we are able to generalize from those few representatives to achieve competitive results to the expert designed rules used in existing IDS Camnep.

Keywords: Intrusion detection · Random forests · NetFlow · Camnep

1 Introduction

Intrusion detection systems analyse network traffic data with the goal to reveal malicious activities and incidents. In this paper we refer to an existing solution for intrusion detection, a multistage collective network behavior analysis system called Camnep [22]. The strategy of Camnep is to monitor high volume traffic networks for incidents, based on statistical information aggregated from publicly accessible parts of connections, i.e network flows or *NetFlows* (Section 3), utilizing variety of techniques from rules to statistical modeling. To assess maliciousness of incidents the system needs to extract higher-level information from lower-level data by constructing so called *events* from the individual NetFlows. Aggregating NetFlows to meaningful entities is an open problem and existing solutions rely mostly on standards and handmade rules designed by domain experts.

The goal of this paper is to provide adaptive machine learning model, capable to generalize from an extremely small number of available true attack representatives, with accuracy close to the expert designed process presented in Camnep.

© IFIP International Federation for Information Processing 2015
S. Latré et al. (Eds.): AIMS 2015, LNCS 9122, pp. 73–86, 2015.
DOI: 10.1007/978-3-319-20034-7_9

To that aim, we first introduce a fast scalable heuristic procedure for the extraction of generic events from NetFlow traffic (Section 4). Second, we propose an enhanced Random-Forest-based learning model (Section 5) utilizing the small number of available ground truth samples of particular incident types, with the help of a large number of samples generated from background traffic by the heuristic procedure. The performance of the learned model to identify intrusions is evaluated against Camnep on the same traffic data, and a correspondence of the two methods is analyzed (Section 6).

2   Related Work

The amount of network generated data and progress in the area of machine learning suggest for development of automatic and adaptive solutions to address the intrusion detection problem, and there has been a wide variety of machine learning approaches proposed to tackle IDS issues [28]. Related works utilize decision trees to learn explicit knowledge [15], and unsupervised methods using clustering as an inherent part of network traffic analysis [16]. In some latest works, even distributed, robust approaches utilizing strategies from trust modeling and game theory were introduced [2].

The most relevant works, assuming the nature of our dataset, include one-class anomaly detection methods for IDS [20], and semi-supervised approaches for traffic classification [9]. From the learning point of view, the most related works include utilizing Random Forests algorithm to build intrusion patterns [8] or to detect anomalies through the random forest outlier measure [29].

However, in real world practice, there are numerous issues affiliated with an online use of machine learning models on actual networks, and majority of the IDS currently in use are still either rule, or expert system based [18], providing the advantage of interpretability. A somewhat hybrid approach is presented in Camnep [22], which combines expert rules for information and feature extraction on the lower stages, with data mining, classification, agent techniques and trust modeling in the final stages [23].

A number of the related works refer to a popular dataset created in 1999 named KDD'99 [19], published by Defence Advanced Research Projects Agency (DARPA). Although it was a step forward in comparing and evaluating IDS approaches, this work has received a lot of critique for including flaws in many statistical respects [27], limitations that are inherited from the DARPA datasets [17], and is widely considered outdated. While problems with the KDD'99 dataset are well-known, in this paper we refer to a real-use IDS Camnep [22], processing recent university traffic, instead of KDD'99, in a widely used NetFlow format to guide and evaluate ourselves, so that we can work with actual incidents and provide feedback relevant to the system.

In contrast with most previous works on detection we take a rather different approach than just classifying preprocessed standalone connections with features, that are not always present in practice, as we address the problem on an event layer, built on top of the NetFlow records. The main contribution of this work is then the joint approach to the detection problem, aggregating flows into events and leveraging the potentially unlimited source of useful background samples (Section 4) for the respectively customized tree ensemble learning model (Section 5.1). We finally evaluate our model against real-use IDS [22], while utilizing the NetFlow standard format, collected from in-line university network probes, all in actual development with Cisco research.

3 Traffic Data

The traffic data we work with were collected from local university (CTU) network during a period of one week. In its raw form the data consist of elementary information aggregated from network packets, which we refer to in this paper as NetFlows. It is a unidirectional component of TCP (UDP, ICMP equivalent) identified by shared source and destination addresses and ports, together with the protocol, captured within the frame of activity defined by a timeout mechanism. The NetFlow format was introduced on Cisco routers to give the ability to collect IP network traffic as it enters or exits an interface, and it is a tuple of:

Start, Duration, Protocol, src-IP, src-Port, dest-IP, dest-Port, Flags,
#Packets, #Bytes

This format is widely adopted for security event logging and a number of affiliated disciplines[12,24]. As a comprehensible unit of network communication with a number of high level features, many IDS works built their detection capabilities on the NetFlow level [26], but generally the incidents and attacks may consist of a multitude of NetFlows. Such sets of flows are commonly called *events*. In addition to information carried by individual flows, events display more complex aggregated properties that cannot be perceived on the individual flow level [2].

Example 1. For a simplistic instance consider a sequence of flows aiming at a particular endpoint port 22. If each of the flows is to be analyzed separately, it can easily be considered as a regular ssh communication request. Yet when we group those flows, according to their properties, such as the destination endpoint, we can explore potential malicious ssh-cracking behavior from the distributed plurality of small similar flows checking the same ssh endpoint during a short time-scope, possibly transferring a considerable amount of data back afterwards.

In this paper, we work with two sources of available data: *ground truth events* and *background traffic flows*. Ground truth events represent attacks evaluated and confirmed by a domain expert and constitute our only source of positive training examples. They are quite scarce as there are only dozens of ground truth events collected. The particular samples of attacks in our ground-truth events include various types of port-scan behavior and samples of ssh-cracking. We are aware that the particularities of these two types of attacks introduce bias into the model, making it possibly hard to generalize over different types of attacks, especially those with more complex network behavior. Nevertheless, for the sake of clarity we refer to these samples in the rest of the paper as generally the *malicious events* or *attacks*.

Background traffic flows is then a large collection of all flows from a snapshot of the local university network traffic. Events occurring within this collection are not available and yet need to be determined (Section 4). Also the true nature of the underlying background traffic is unknown, but believed to be generally legit. Most of the events probably correspond to harmless activities but some of them may also correspond to attacks. Since, in the end, we will need to evaluate how accurately our learned models are able to detect attacks and, more specifically, how close they can get to the performance of particular Camnep rules, we will proceed as follows. In the training phase, we will always work only with the ground truth events and with the unlabeled background traffic but in the testing phase, we will label the background traffic using Camnep and evaluate the accuracy of the learned models using its output labeled test-set events. In the rest of the paper, we will refer to the background traffic events labeled as malicious by Camnep as the *system samples*.

Naturally, the use of labels obtained using Camnep as a proxy for the true labeling has its drawbacks, particularly that a model which could detect the same set of malicious events as Camnep perfectly and on top of that also some missed malicious events would be considered worse than a model which would just perfectly mimic Camnep. However, there is no simple remedy for this problem except a laborious confirmation of the detected discrepancies by a domain expert, which is costly and time-consuming and which we therefore did not perform for this initial study (but which we plan to do in the future).

4   Event Extraction

As we mentioned, the extraction of events from background flows is a crucial step in the detection of malicious behavior. Unfortunately, there is no general prescription of how an event should be formed based on the properties of the underlying flow set, and common approaches (including Camnep) thus rely on some form of flow clustering [5]. Whatever the underlying events look like, we need to miss as few malicious samples as possible, and thus we generally want the event extraction procedure not to be picky about what constitutes an event. For this reason we restrain from using standard clustering algorithms, employing pair-wise similarity metric defined on the flow level, as they would introduce a bias, while assigning each flow into a single cluster, possibly causing some of the attacks to be missed. In other words, in this stage we want to generally maximize recall of events and leave the burden of selecting the proper malicious ones on classifiers trained to do so based on past data. On the other hand, we also cannot extract all subsets of background flows as events because there would be an astronomical number of them. Therefore, the way the background event samples are constructed comes from generic rules, capturing only very general constraints on what is and what is not an event. Most of these rules can be

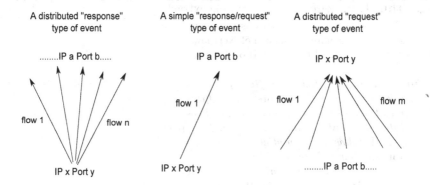

Fig. 1. Illustration of event structure type behavior variations as induced by the use of background event extraction rules

understood as a parallel to the basic NetFlow/IPFIX aggregation features [7], but they operate on top of the Netflow level, creating more complex aggregates with considerable amount of redundancy for the sake of proper event recall maximization (while surely extracting a number of false events, too). We design the extraction rules as follows.

endpoint rules
1. all flows share the same source IP and source port
2. all flows share the same source IP and destination port
3. all flows share the same destination IP and source port
4. all flows share the same destination IP and destination port

similarity rules
1. all flows share the same protocol
2. all flow sizes, i.e. number of bytes transferred, are similar
3. all the flows are close enough in time

Each of the subsets of the above set of 4 address rules $\{1..4\}$, combined together with the full set $\{1, 2, 3\}$ of similarity rules, constitute a prescription on how to extract event from the used background traffic netflow data. Applying all of these combinations exhaustively on the data, as described in Algorithm 1, we can extract high diversity of network events.

In the background event extraction process, the incoming NetFlow sequence is simply being split into discrete time intervals to consider the events within, which is sort of a standard in network traffic monitoring and analysis [25]. The sets of flows are then stored in clusters, growing as the new NetFlows are coming from the traffic. The incoming flows are checked against the rules that define a mask on the flow endpoints and other static properties, such as protocol in our simple scenario. Each of the flow clusters also stores a number of properties such as the values of common endpoints, average size of flows, flags, etc. These properties are maintained during the whole process, resulting into events that represent diverse

---

Algorithm 1. Background event sample extraction

1: $ruleBase \leftarrow$ the rule combinations for generic events
2: $flows \leftarrow$ the incoming sequence of NetFlow
3: $winSize \leftarrow$ maximal time spread of flows
4:
5: **function** DISTRIBUTEFLOWS($flows$)   ▷ flow distribution
6:    $minTime \leftarrow$ time of the first $flow \in flows$
7:    $maxTime \leftarrow$ time of the last $flow \in flows$
8:    $intervalCount \leftarrow (maxTime - minTime)/winSize$
9:    $flowWindows \leftarrow emptySet$
10:   **for all** $flow \in flows$ **do**
11:       $idx = (flow.time - minTime)/winSize$
12:       $flowWindows_{idx} = flowWindows_{idx} \cup flow$
13:   **return** $flowWindows$
14:
15: $flowWindows \leftarrow$ **DistributeFlows**($flows$)
16:
17: **procedure** EXTRACTEVENTS   ▷ flow aggregation
18:   **for all** $flowWindow \in flowWindows$ **do**
19:       **for all** $rule \in ruleBase$ **do**
20:           **for all** $flow \in flowWindow$ **do**
21:               **if** $flow.properties \subseteq rule.properties$ **then**
22:                   **JoinClusters**($flow, rule$)
23:
24: $events \leftarrow emptySet$
25:
26: **procedure** JOINCLUSTERS($flow, rule$)   ▷ rule checking
27:   $added \leftarrow false$
28:   **for all** $cluster \in events$ **do**
29:       $endpoints = rule.endpoints \wedge cluster.endpoints$
30:       **if** $endpoints \subseteq flow.endpoints$ **then**
31:           **if** $flow.size \approx cluster.averageSize$ **then**
32:               $cluster = cluster \cup flow$
33:               $endpoints = endpoints \cap flow.endpoints$
34:               $cluster.endpoints = endpoints$
35:               $added \leftarrow true$
36:   **if** $\neg added$ **then**
37:       $nC = \{flow\}$
38:       $nC.endpoints = flow.endpoints \wedge rule.endpoints$
39:       $events = events \cup nC$

---

network behavior, including variety of structural configurations of events, such as those depicted in Figure 1, which are similar to *graphlet* patterns explored in other works on flow traffic classification [13].

We note that the configuration of this exhaustive extraction strategy ensures that every event detected by Camnep from the same traffic data will also occur as some event, or a subpart thereof, in the extracted background-traffic event set, and so the proper event recall is truly maximal. Moreover, various valid parts of such an event might get extracted as well.

Example 2. For instance, in our setting all single flow ssh requests to an endpoint server within a short time period will get extracted as a compact "many-to-one ssh-requests" event, yet some of those requests might get grouped by the source IP only, as well as all of these single requests will again stand as separate ssh-request events in the final background event dataset.

This does not mean that all flow subsets of an event are extracted, but generally rather those maximal sets that exhibit some interesting and common behavior of flows, according to their structural and other properties, as restricted by the generic prescription rules and the nature of the traffic itself.

5 Learning

The goal of learning a classifier from the network traffic data is to automatically generalize knowledge from a small number of ground truth attacks available, with an accuracy comparable to that of a human domain expert. For that we use similar, relatively simple and intelligible representation of an event as a set of 30 features calculated from standard aggregation functions applied over the sets of contained flows and their attributes, such as count of flows, average of #packets, standard deviation of #bytes, etc.

There is a wide variety of different methods for training classifiers from data. However, as it turns out, the characteristics of the network traffic data which we study in this paper make a straightforward application of off-the-shelf machine learning tools a bit problematic. The two main reasons for this are as follows. First, we have labels only for the positive examples (the ground-truth malicious events) and we only know about the other larger part of the data coming from the background traffic that the fraction of positive examples is extremely small. Second, the datasets which we work with are highly class-skewed, with a skew usually of several orders of magnitude (the ratio of $1 : 10^5$ is easily possible in this domain) as total majority of the events in the background traffic correspond to normal activities.

Besides straightforward approaches, such as considering the background traffic globally negative, there are remedies to tackle this problem. In particular, there is variety of anomaly detection approaches, utilizing notably one class classifiers [14], and semi-supervised strategies, exploiting the unlabeled majority of data through the few labeled samples and some a priori assumptions [11]. A similarly motivated approach is to exploit the assumption that malicious events are rare and similar to each other, which would ideally mean that they occupy small neighborhoods of ground-truth malicious events in the feature space. We further explore this intuition through a method based on ensembling techniques.

5.1 Subsampled Random Forests

One of the best-performing [10] machine learning algorithms these days is the Random Forest [4]. The algorithm creates an ensemble of decision trees by bagging. In each iteration of the Random Forest algorithm, a bag of examples is randomly selected by sampling with replacements the same number of examples as is in the original dataset. Then, one tree is learned upon each such resampled dataset where, in the learning process, the features to be used in a split node are only selected from a randomly sampled subset of features. The output of a learned Random Forest classifier is computed as the average of votes of the individual trees in the ensemble. The classification of a test example is then performed by comparing the output of the random forest classifier to a selected threshold. Thus, by decreasing the threshold, one can usually increase the number of true positives but also, at the same time, the number of false positives. The output of Random Forest can also be thought of as the confidence of classifying an example as positive. It can so be used to rank events from most suspicious to least suspicious.

However, Random Forest itself is not well suited for learning from imbalanced datasets. There have been two main remedies proposed to tackle this problem [6], one of them based on cost sensitive learning, and the other on the use of sampling. The cost sensitive methods performed poorly in our scenario and thus we further explored the sampling methods that are able to target a deeper issue. The issue is that when the number of background-traffic examples becomes really large, it is no longer just a matter of balancing the cost thresholds, as the trees in the ensemble become very correlated in the sense that they share very similar decision boundaries, and therefore the output of the learned forests will be equal for a majority of events, making it impossible to reasonably rank them by their suspiciousness. To solve this problem, we utilize a simple modification of the original majority class subsampling strategy [6], somewhat similar to [3], stated as follows. When sampling the positive examples of which there are only a few instances, we follow the normal strategy and sample with replacements a set of the same size as the positive set, but when sampling the negative examples we sample a smaller set (also with replacements) with the subsampling ratio given as a parameter. Intuitively this simple strategy should increase the variability among the trees.

Example 3. An illustration of the intuition giving a rationale for the above method is shown in Figure 2. Here, the examples are 1-dimensional and can acquire values from 0 to 1. There are 10^5 learning examples sampled from the uniform distribution on the interval $(0, 1)$. The examples to the left from 0.1 threshold are classified as positive and the rest as negative. We train a bagged ensemble of threshold decision rules on this data. The dash-dotted line in Figure 2 corresponds to outputs of an ensemble obtained by conventional bagging, whereas the solid curve corresponds to outputs of an ensemble trained by the method in which negative examples are always subsampled for each bootstrap sample. We can notice that the subsampled case still gives the same output for the examples in the area where positive samples occur, which is a desirable behavior in the case of expert-labeled ground-truth positive events. On the other hand, the output decays more slowly in the area of negative examples and thus allows us to rank them. We expect that a similar effect takes place while sub-

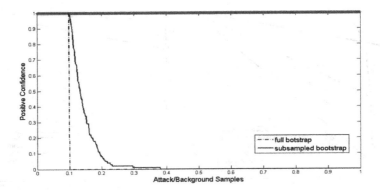

Fig. 2. Illustration of the intuition for the subsampled random forest method

sampling the negative examples in the random forest model. The results of our experiments performed in Section 6 actually suggest that this is indeed the case.

The motivation for the subsampling method employed in this work is different from the motivation for the methods developed in literature for dealing with imbalanced datasets using Random Forests [6,3]. In our case, what we need to achieve is to have different output values for as many examples as possible, so that we can rank the events by our confidence that they are attacks and not a normal traffic. We also know class labels of only a subset of positive examples and no class labels for negative examples. On the other hand, in existing works, the main motivation is to improve classification performance when all class labels are known.

6 Evaluation

We performed several experiments in order to evaluate the ability of different types of models to detect malicious events in the data. For training, we only used the ground truth and the background traffic data. For testing on separate test-sets, we created labeled events using the Camnep system utilizing the expert rules. As described in Section 3, this means that some of the false positive events detected by some classifiers may in fact correspond to true positives, and so our evaluation is a bit skewed towards pessimism, but there is no other tractable way of obtaining labels for the events in the background traffic part of our dataset. Moreover, as we will see, some classifiers (notably the subsampled random forests) are able to obtain some very good ROC curves, which indirectly confirms accurateness of the labeling provided by Camnep.

6.1 State of the Art Classifiers

The first logical step, after performing initial data exploration experiments to justify the machine learning approach, was to test off-the-shelf, state-of-the-art

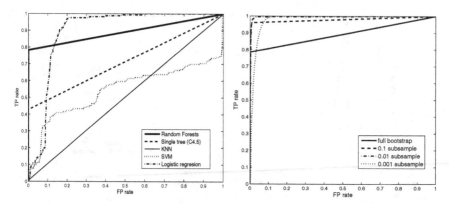

Fig. 3. A comparison of the selected state-of-the-art classifiers with ROC analysis, where Random Forest and a single tree model dominate the beginning of the ROC(left). Enhancement of Random Forest with the introduced subsampling technique boosts the performance further(right), with the subsample ratio varying from a full bootstrap(default Random Forest) to 0.001 subsample.

machine learning algorithms. The algorithms we tested were decision trees, random forests, support vector machines, logistic regression and k-nearest neighbors. Recall that the extreme class-skew of the dataset can render some otherwise very good conventional algorithms unusable for our problem. Although some remedies could be found for those, the instant superior performance of trees and their ensembles, especially in the beginning of ROC, as displayed for comparison in Figure 3 (left), led us to exploit further in their direction.

6.2   Subsampled Random Forests

The performance of Random Forests, although superior to other standard approaches, was still not satisfactory. Most of the attacks were correctly classified right from the start, i.e. with very low false positive rates, but the rest of the system attacks was not covered until the false positive rates reached unbearable levels (Figure 3, left). On the other hand, we noticed that these system attack samples were possible to be in covered in some way, e.g., by generalized linear regressions. However, we could expect such behavior based on the intuition presented in Section 5.1. There we explained why subsampling the background traffic in the process of learning random forest classifiers should be beneficial in settings like ours, where there are a few positive examples and a large number of unlabeled samples, most of which are probably negative.

We have tested various subsample ratios as parameters for the subsampling strategy, and the resulting influence on the ROC performance of the tree ensemble can be seen in Figure 3 (right). Generally, we can note that the full bootstrap performance, equal to the performance of the default Random Forest, is always improved by the introduction of subsampling in terms of the area under the ROC curve. The decreasing sizes of bootstraps are gradually progressing towards higher true positive rates

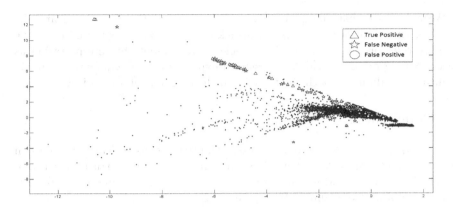

Fig. 4. CLS visualization of the model behavior by the means of ROC characteristics

at the expense of increasing the false positives under different paces. Although the results are not conclusive for choosing a generally optimal sub-sample ratio, we further favor the rates from around 0.01 to 0.1, providing a satisfactory compromise between the true and false positives.

6.3   Model Analysis

We have shown that an automatic method is able to learn a model with a performance similar to the expert rules designed in Camnep. To further evaluate and interpret the behavior of the learned model, we visualize the results in a similar fashion to ROC characteristics as follows. We mark the system attack samples covered by the model as true positives, those that were not covered as false negatives, and possibly regular traffic covered as false positives. All these characteristics were then recorded for varying classification threshold scores. Using a fast dimension reduction technique called Calibrated Least Squares (CLS) [21], that was best able to visually distinguish these samples, we display the results, for a chosen threshold, in Figure 4. From the projection we identify that the most significant dimensions are mostly correlated with the overall size of events, which is generally reflected in the expert rules, too. To search for some closer correspondence with Camnep rules, we further explore the interpretability of the model by extracting a single tree model from the ensemble, using a learning technique introduced in [1]. For the interpretation, the extracted tree had to be rapidly pruned, which renders its node decisions partially inaccurate. Nevertheless, from the splits in the nodes of the tree, we were able to identify a number of patterns with an interpretation similar to the original Camnep rules. Some examples of the extracted decisions from the paths commonly leading to malicious-behavior-signed leaves in the tree, are as follows.

- If the percentage of unique sizes of flows is lower than 40%
- If the average number of packets transferred is lower than 6
- If the shared destination port of flows equals 22
- If the number of unique source ports is greater than 5

We are aware that the generality and accuracy of these decisions are disputable, and some bias towards the attack samples used is exhibited (e.g., the 22 port rule for ssh-cracking). Nevertheless, we present the interpretation as an interesting option to validate design of expert rules, by which we indirectly confirm the validity of both the model and the original rules used in Camnep.

7   Conclusions

In this paper we presented and analyzed adaptive means to learn an intrusion detection model, from an extremely small number of ground truth attack representatives, with a performance competitive to the expert rule driven process provided in a part of Camnep IDS system [22].

To capture more complex aggregation properties of the malicious behavior in scope, we addressed the problem on the event level, built on top of the NetFlow layer, for which we introduced a fast, generic, heuristic event extraction procedure. Recognizing the lack of ground truth event samples in the domain of IDS, we utilized this procedure to extract variety of presumably normal event behavior from a given background university NetFlow traffic. With the new extended training sample set, consisting of a few original ground truth attacks and essentially unlimited number of background events, we presented machine learning methods to compare against the output of Camnep on the same traffic.

To surpass the results of the state-of-the-art algorithms tested, we introduced a novel random-forest-based subsampling method for tuning an ensemble tree classifier, with a semi-supervised motivation, to account for the imbalanced nature of the data. This method is based on bootstrap subsampling, suppressing the correlation of individual trees, w.r.t. class frequencies, and by its means we increased the ensemble performance beyond the scope of regularly used tuning, such as sample or misclassification weighting. The results of the experiments performed suggested for the benefits of our bootstrap subsampling method, the overall ability to learn to detect the attacks from the traffic in scope, and also indirectly confirmed validity of the approach and particular rules from Camnep.

Acknowledgements. This work was supported by Cisco sponsored research project "Modelling Network Traffic with Relational Features", and Czech Technical University internal grant SGS14/079/OHK3/1T/13. Part of this work was done while the second author was with KU Leuven where he was supported by Jan Ramon's ERC Starting Grant 240186 "MiGraNT: Mining Graphs and Networks, a Theory-based approach".

References

1. Van Assche, A., Blockeel, H.: Seeing the forest through the trees: Learning a comprehensible model from an ensemble. In: Kok, J.N., Koronacki, J., Lopez de Mantaras, R., Matwin, S., Mladenič, D., Skowron, A. (eds.) ECML 2007. LNCS (LNAI), vol. 4701, pp. 418–429. Springer, Heidelberg (2007)
2. Bartos, K., Rehak, M.: Trust-based solution for robust self-configuration of distributed intrusion detection systems, pp. 121–126 (2012)

3. Błaszczyński, J., Stefanowski, J., Idkowiak, L.: Extending bagging for imbalanced data. In: Burduk, R., Jackowski, K., Kurzynski, M., Wozniak, M., Zolnierek, A. (eds.) CORES 2013. AISC, vol. 226, pp. 269–278. Springer, Heidelberg (2013)
4. Breiman, L.: Random forests. Machine Learning 45(1), 5–32 (2001)
5. Chaudhary, U.K., Papapanagiotou, I., Devetsikiotis, M.: Flow classification using clustering and association rule mining. In: 2010 15th IEEE International Workshop on Computer Aided Modeling, Analysis and Design of Communication Links and Networks (CAMAD), pp. 76–80. IEEE (2010)
6. Chen, C., Liaw, A., Breiman, L.: Using random forest to learn imbalanced data. University of California, Berkeley (2004)
7. Claise, B.: Cisco systems netflow services export version 9 (September 2004)
8. Elbasiony, R.M., Sallam, E.A., Eltobely, T.E., Fahmy, M.M.: A hybrid network intrusion detection framework based on random forests and weighted k-means. Ain Shams Engineering Journal 4(4), 753–762 (2013)
9. Erman, J., Mahanti, A., Arlitt, M., Cohen, I., Williamson, C.: Offline/realtime traffic classification using semi-supervised learning. Performance Evaluation 64(9), 1194–1213 (2007)
10. Fernández-Delgado, M., Cernadas, E., Barro, S., Amorim, D.: Do we need hundreds of classifiers to solve real world classification problems? The Journal of Machine Learning Research 15(1), 3133–3181 (2014)
11. Huang, T.M., Kecman, V.: Semi-supervised learning from unbalanced labeled data–an improvement. In: Negoita, M.G., Howlett, R.J., Jain, L.C. (eds.) KES 2004. LNCS (LNAI), vol. 3215, pp. 802–808. Springer, Heidelberg (2004)
12. Jiang, H., Moore, A.W., Ge, Z., Jin, S., Wang, J.: Lightweight application classification for network management. In: Proceedings of the 2007 SIGCOMM Workshop on Internet Network Management, pp. 299–304. ACM (2007)
13. Karagiannis, T., Papagiannaki, K., Faloutsos, M.: Blinc: multilevel traffic classification in the dark. In: ACM SIGCOMM Computer Communication Review, vol. 35, pp. 229–240. ACM (2005)
14. Khan, S.S., Madden, M.G.: A survey of recent trends in one class classification. In: Coyle, L., Freyne, J. (eds.) AICS 2009. LNCS (LNAI), vol. 6206, pp. 188–197. Springer, Heidelberg (2010)
15. Laskov, P., Düssel, P., Schäfer, C., Rieck, K.: Learning intrusion detection: supervised or unsupervised? In: Roli, F., Vitulano, S. (eds.) ICIAP 2005. LNCS, vol. 3617, pp. 50–57. Springer, Heidelberg (2005)
16. Leung, K., Leckie, C.: Unsupervised anomaly detection in network intrusion detection using clusters, pp. 333–342 (2005)
17. McHugh, J.: Testing intrusion detection systems: a critique of the 1998 and 1999 darpa intrusion detection system evaluations as performed by lincoln laboratory. ACM Transactions on Information and system Security 3(4), 262–294 (2000)
18. Mizutani, M., Takeda, K., Murai, J.: Behavior rule based intrusion detection, pp. 57–58 (2009)
19. Adetunmbi, A., Olusola, A.S.: Oladele, and Daramola O Abosede. Analysis of kdd99 intrusion detection dataset for selection of relevance features. In: Proceedings of the World Congress on Engineering and Computer Science, vol. 1, pp. 20–22 (2010)
20. Perdisci, R., Gu, V., Lee, W.: Using an ensemble of one-class svm classifiers to harden payload-based anomaly detection systems. In: Sixth International Conference on Data Mining, ICDM 2006, pp. 488–498. IEEE (2006)
21. Pevný, T., Ker, A.D.: The challenges of rich features in universal steganalysis (2013)

22. Rehak, M., Pechoucek, M., Celeda, P., Novotny, J., Minarik, P.: Camnep: agent-based network intrusion detection system, pp. 133–136 (2008)
23. Rehak, M., Pechoucek, M., Grill, M., Stiborek, J., Bartoš, K., Celeda, P.: Adaptive multiagent system for network traffic monitoring. IEEE Intelligent Systems (3), 16–25 (2009)
24. Rossi, D., Valenti, S.: Fine-grained traffic classification with netflow data, pp. 479–483 (2010)
25. So-In, C.: A survey of network traffic monitoring and analysis tools. Cse 576m Computer System Analysis Project, Washington University in St. Louis (2009)
26. Sperotto, A., Schaffrath, G., Sadre, R., Morariu, C., Pras, A., Stiller, B.: An overview of ip flow-based intrusion detection. IEEE Communications Surveys Tutorials 12(3), 343–356 (2010)
27. Tavallaee, M., Bagheri, E., Lu, W., Ghorbani, A.-A.: A detailed analysis of the kdd cup 99 data set (2009)
28. Tsai, C.-F., Hsu, Y.-F., Lin, C.-Y., Lin, W.-Y.: Intrusion detection by machine learning: A review. Expert Systems with Applications 36(10), 11994–12000 (2009)
29. Zhang, J., Zulkernine, M., Haque, A.: Random-forests-based network intrusion detection systems. IEEE Transactions on Systems, Man, and Cybernetics, Part C: Applications and Reviews 38(5), 649–659 (2008)

22. Rehak, M., Pechoucek, M., Celeda, P., Novotny, J., Minarik, P.: Camnep: agent-based network intrusion detection system, pp. 133–136 (2008)
23. Rehak, M., Pechoucek, M., Grill, M., Stiborek, J., Bartoš, K., Celeda, P.: Adaptive multiagent system for network traffic monitoring. IEEE Intelligent Systems (3), 16–25 (2009)
24. Rossi, D., Valenti, S.: Fine-grained traffic classification with netflow data, pp. 479–483 (2010)
25. So-In, C.: A survey of network traffic monitoring and analysis tools. Cse 576m Computer System Analysis Project, Washington University in St. Louis (2009)
26. Sperotto, A., Schaffrath, G., Sadre, R., Morariu, C., Pras, A., Stiller, B.: An overview of ip flow-based intrusion detection. IEEE Communications Surveys Tutorials 12(3), 343–356 (2010)
27. Tavallaee, M., Bagheri, E., Lu, W., Ghorbani, A.-A.: A detailed analysis of the kdd cup 99 data set (2009)
28. Tsai, C.-F., Hsu, Y.-F., Lin, C.-Y., Lin, W.-Y.: Intrusion detection by machine learning: A review. Expert Systems with Applications 36(10), 11994–12000 (2009)
29. Zhang, J., Zulkernine, M., Haque, A.: Random-forests-based network intrusion detection systems. IEEE Transactions on Systems, Man, and Cybernetics, Part C: Applications and Reviews 38(5), 649–659 (2008)

3. Błaszczyński, J., Stefanowski, J., Idkowiak, Ł.: Extending bagging for imbalanced data. In: Burduk, R., Jackowski, K., Kurzynski, M., Wozniak, M., Zolnierek, A. (eds.) CORES 2013. AISC, vol. 226, pp. 269–278. Springer, Heidelberg (2013)
4. Breiman, L.: Random forests. Machine Learning 45(1), 5–32 (2001)
5. Chaudhary, U.K., Papapanagiotou, I., Devetsikiotis, M.: Flow classification using clustering and association rule mining. In: 2010 15th IEEE International Workshop on Computer Aided Modeling, Analysis and Design of Communication Links and Networks (CAMAD), pp. 76–80. IEEE (2010)
6. Chen, C., Liaw, A., Breiman, L.: Using random forest to learn imbalanced data. University of California, Berkeley (2004)
7. Claise, B.: Cisco systems netflow services export version 9 (September 2004)
8. Elbasiony, R.M., Sallam, E.A., Eltobely, T.E., Fahmy, M.M.: A hybrid network intrusion detection framework based on random forests and weighted k-means. Ain Shams Engineering Journal 4(4), 753–762 (2013)
9. Erman, J., Mahanti, A., Arlitt, M., Cohen, I., Williamson, C.: Offline/realtime traffic classification using semi-supervised learning. Performance Evaluation 64(9), 1194–1213 (2007)
10. Fernández-Delgado, M., Cernadas, E., Barro, S., Amorim, D.: Do we need hundreds of classifiers to solve real world classification problems? The Journal of Machine Learning Research 15(1), 3133–3181 (2014)
11. Huang, T.M., Kecman, V.: Semi-supervised learning from unbalanced labeled data– an improvement. In: Negoita, M.G., Howlett, R.J., Jain, L.C. (eds.) KES 2004. LNCS (LNAI), vol. 3215, pp. 802–808. Springer, Heidelberg (2004)
12. Jiang, H., Moore, A.W., Ge, Z., Jin, S., Wang, J.: Lightweight application classification for network management. In: Proceedings of the 2007 SIGCOMM Workshop on Internet Network Management, pp. 299–304. ACM (2007)
13. Karagiannis, T., Papagiannaki, K., Faloutsos, M.: Blinc: multilevel traffic classification in the dark. In: ACM SIGCOMM Computer Communication Review, vol. 35, pp. 229–240. ACM (2005)
14. Khan, S.S., Madden, M.G.: A survey of recent trends in one class classification. In: Coyle, L., Freyne, J. (eds.) AICS 2009. LNCS (LNAI), vol. 6206, pp. 188–197. Springer, Heidelberg (2010)
15. Laskov, P., Düssel, P., Schäfer, C., Rieck, K.: Learning intrusion detection: supervised or unsupervised? In: Roli, F., Vitulano, S. (eds.) ICIAP 2005. LNCS, vol. 3617, pp. 50–57. Springer, Heidelberg (2005)
16. Leung, K., Leckie, C.: Unsupervised anomaly detection in network intrusion detection using clusters, pp. 333–342 (2005)
17. McHugh, J.: Testing intrusion detection systems: a critique of the 1998 and 1999 darpa intrusion detection system evaluations as performed by lincoln laboratory. ACM Transactions on Information and system Security 3(4), 262–294 (2000)
18. Mizutani, M., Takeda, K., Murai, J.: Behavior rule based intrusion detection, pp. 57–58 (2009)
19. Adetunmbi, A., Olusola, A.S.: Oladele, and Daramola O Abosede. Analysis of kdd99 intrusion detection dataset for selection of relevance features. In: Proceedings of the World Congress on Engineering and Computer Science, vol. 1, pp. 20–22 (2010)
20. Perdisci, R., Gu, V., Lee, W.: Using an ensemble of one-class svm classifiers to harden payload-based anomaly detection systems. In: Sixth International Conference on Data Mining, ICDM 2006, pp. 488–498. IEEE (2006)
21. Pevný, T., Ker, A.D.: The challenges of rich features in universal steganalysis (2013)

Using Application-Aware Flow Monitoring
for SIP Fraud Detection

Tomas Cejka[1]([⊠]), Vaclav Bartos[2], Lukas Truxa[1], and Hana Kubatova[3]

[1] CESNET, a.l.e., Zikova 4, 160 00, Prague 6, Czech Republic
cejkat@cesnet.cz
[2] Faculty of Information Technology, Brno University of Technology, Bozetechova 2,
Brno, Czech Republic
ibartosv@fit.vutbr.cz
[3] CTU in Prague, FIT, Thakurova 9, 160 00, Prague 6, Czech Republic
kubatova@fit.cvut.cz

Abstract. Flow monitoring helps to discover many network security
threats targeted to various applications or network protocols. In this paper, we show usage of the flow data for analysis of a Voice over IP (VoIP)
traffic and a threat detection. A traditionally used flow record is insufficient for this purpose and therefore it was extended by application-layer
information. In particular, we focus on the Session Initiation Protocol
(SIP) and the type of a toll-fraud in which an attacker tries to exploit
poor configuration of a private branch exchange (PBX). The attacker's
motivation is to make unauthorized calls to PSTN numbers that are
usually charged at high rates and owned by the attacker. As a result,
a successful attack can cause a significant financial loss to the owner of
PBX. We propose a method for stream-wise and near real-time analysis of the SIP traffic and detection of the described threat. The method
was implemented as a module of the Nemea system and deployed on
a backbone network. It was evaluated using simulated as well as real
attacks.

1   Introduction

Computer networks are a multifunctional communication channel used by various different applications. The example of such an application that is studied in
this paper is the telephone service – the Voice over IP (VoIP) technology. This,
as well as many other applications, is often considered to be critically important
for users. It is therefore important to have effective ways for quick detection
of any problems, including security threats. This often means a necessity for
monitoring and analysis of the traffic. A common approach allowing situational
awareness even in high speed networks is the usage of flow monitoring.

Traditional flow monitoring provides data extracted from packet headers up
to the transport layer. Therefore, it provides information about IP addresses,
TCP/UDP ports, TCP flags or ICMP message types in form of flow records.
The flow records also contain statistics such as number of packets, number of

© IFIP International Federation for Information Processing 2015
S. Latré et al. (Eds.): AIMS 2015, LNCS 9122, pp. 87–99, 2015.
DOI: 10.1007/978-3-319-20034-7_10

transferred bytes and information about observation time. However, there is no detailed information about application layer protocols in the flow records.

The traditional flow record is sufficient for many purposes, including detection of several types of malicious traffic. For example, port scanning and SYN flood attacks are easy to detect using only these basic flow data, since these attacks have clearly distinguishable characteristics on network and transport layers. Even some attacks on application layer, such as dictionary attacks on SSH, can be detected using basic flow data with proper algorithms [7]. However, this is not always possible or it may be very difficult and unreliable. For some kinds of malicious traffic, knowledge of additional information from the application layer is necessary for reliable detection.

Fortunately, application awareness has been implemented into some flow exporters in the last years, usually in the form of plugins [9]. Such exporters inspect packet payload, extract information from headers of application layer protocols and add this information into flow records. The *extended flow records* can contain e.g. URLs, response codes from HTTP, or domain names from DNS requests along with common features of the flow record. The flow records are then transferred to a collector using the IPFIX protocol [3].

The extension of flow records by application layer information was added mainly to allow more detailed statistics about traffic or to support application performance monitoring. However, it can be used for detection of security threats as well. In this paper, we show an example of such a usage.

We focus on monitoring of the VoIP traffic, in particular the Session Initiation Protocol (SIP). Our goal is to detect one of the most common VoIP frauds – the one in which an attacker tries to misuse a poorly secured gateway to the public switched telephone network (PSTN) to make unauthorized calls. Such calls are often made to premium-rate numbers (operated by the attackers) causing significant financial losses to operators of the misused gateway.

According to [4], worldwide losses due to VoIP hacking and calling to premium rate services go to billions of dollars per year. It is one of the most costly fraud types in the telecommunication industry. Therefore, even though successful attacks are not very usual, it is highly important to detect them as soon as possible, before a significant damage is caused.

The rest of this paper is organized as follows. The next section describes the related work. Sec. 3 describes details about the attack on which we focus. Sec. 4 describes the detection method and our implementation of it, followed by Sec. 5 where it is evaluated. Sec. 6 concludes the work.

2   Related Work

Attacks and security threats are an ordinary part of network traffic. There are several different types of attacks that are targeted to VoIP infrastructure. Some possible attacks and vulnerability exploits are shown in [5] by El-Moussa et al. The paper describes denial of service attacks, which are very common in computer networks, or SPAM over internet telephony. Furthermore, the authors mention brute-force attacks against authentication mechanism, which are some-what similar to the prefix-guessing attacks described in this paper. They however do not present any countermeasures or a way of detection of such attacks.

Another work enumerating possible attacks against VoIP technology is a survey by A. Keromytis [12]. Although it summarizes hundreds of papers from the area, there is no mention about the kind of attack we deal with, nor any work using flow measurement to detect security threats in VoIP traffic.

To our best knowledge, the only paper providing a way of detection of toll fraud attempts is [8] by Hoffstadt et al. It is focused on monitoring of VoIP threats using honeypots. The authors describe principle of toll fraud based on hijacking of a SIP account. An attacker that gains a user's identity is able to establish a phone call that can be charged. Discovery of a fraud is based on an off-line analysis of honeypot logs. Even though the authors stated that they observed manual attempts of toll fraud, we are observing automatic brute-force guesses of dialing prefixes. Also, our flow-based approach allows to monitor traffic going to real gateways, not only honeypots, therefore we are able to detect real attacks and possibly raise alerts on the successful ones.

Besides common hardware and software VoIP phones, there are several tools that allow users to communicate over SIP in unusual ways. For example, they allow to craft a request with any values of headers or to perform brute-force attacks automatically. Examples of the tools are [6,11,13,15].

A detailed description of the flow monitoring technology can be found in the article [9] by Hofstede et al. It also contains an overview of available software. The paper [14] by Velan and Celeda introduces the concept of application-aware flow monitoring.

3   Principle of the Phone Call Fraud

The following subsection provides a brief introduction to VoIP telephony and SIP. We focus only on aspects needed to understand the type of fraud discussed in this paper and the proposed detection method; we knowingly leave out many otherwise important details for brevity.

3.1   Short Introduction to SIP

Voice over IP is a technology for transferring voice and multimedial data over computer networks. Session Initiation Protocol (SIP) is the well-known protocol used for initiation, control and termination of VoIP sessions (or calls). The multimedial data are transferred in a separate channel using Real-time Transport Protocol (RTP).

SIP is a protocol based on a request-response transaction model. Every device can act both as a client or as a server. The client creates and sends requests, the server receives and processes them, and generates one or more replies. The high-level architecture consists mostly of end devices (hardware or software phones) and SIP proxy servers. The proxies receive requests for calls, localize called parties and route the requests to them (possibly via other proxies). They also route replies on their way back to the callers. The proxies also provide authentication services and several other tasks, which are out of scope of this short introduction.

There are several types of requests in SIP. The one which is crucial for this work is INVITE. It is used to initiate a new call. As any request in SIP, it carries several headers describing parameters of the request. The most important headers of INVITE request are:

- *Request-URI:* Used for addressing the called party. It is usually in the form sip:user@host, although more complex forms are possible. The *user* part usually consists of user name or phone number and the *host* part is the destination server where the request should be sent to (domain name or IP address).
- *To:* Called party identification.
- *From:* Identification of the caller.
- *Call-ID:* Unique identifier of a call, usually a long random string.

When INVITE is sent by a client to a proxy server, the request is propagated to the destination, possibly via other proxy servers. Responses such as TRYING and RINGING are returned and when the called party eventually indicates that it is ready to establish the call, the OK response is sent to the caller and the multimedia transfer begins. When the connection can not be established for some reason, a reply with corresponding error code is returned.

If a SIP proxy server is deployed in some private organization to serve as a central hub for internal phone communication and as a proxy for communication with outer world, it is usually called a Private Branch Exchange (PBX). These PBXs usually operate with both VoIP as well as classic telephone networks (PSTN), acting as gateways between those two technologies. The following text focuses on misuse of such gateways.

3.2   Principle of the Fraud

Depending on configuration a PBX may allow users to make VoIP calls to PSTN numbers by setting the destination user ID in an INVITE request to the called number prepended by a special prefix. For example, to call a PSTN number 555-555-0123 a SIP call to 995555550123@example.com needs to be performed, assuming that the gateway is located at example.com and it has "99" configured as the prefix for PSTN calls.

The attack is based on finding poorly secured PBXs and using them to make fraudulent calls to PSTN. Motivations to make such calls may differ, but the common one is to gain money by calling to paid services. This is outlined in Fig. 1. The attacker first loans a premium-rate phone number[1], usually in a foreign country and via some intermediary company. Any calls to that number generate revenue for the attacker. Computers controlled by the attacker are then instructed to find open PBXs and make fake calls via them. When a call is

---

[1]   *I. e.* a number which is charged at a high rate in favour of the line operator.

replies on their way back to the callers. The proxies also provide authentication services and several other tasks, which are out of scope of this short introduction.

There are several types of requests in SIP. The one which is crucial for this work is INVITE. It is used to initiate a new call. As any request in SIP, it carries several headers describing parameters of the request. The most important headers of INVITE request are:

- *Request-URI:* Used for addressing the called party. It is usually in the form sip:user@host, although more complex forms are possible. The *user* part usually consists of user name or phone number and the *host* part is the destination server where the request should be sent to (domain name or IP address).
- *To:* Called party identification.
- *From:* Identification of the caller.
- *Call-ID:* Unique identifier of a call, usually a long random string.

When INVITE is sent by a client to a proxy server, the request is propagated to the destination, possibly via other proxy servers. Responses such as TRYING and RINGING are returned and when the called party eventually indicates that it is ready to establish the call, the OK response is sent to the caller and the multimedia transfer begins. When the connection can not be established for some reason, a reply with corresponding error code is returned.

If a SIP proxy server is deployed in some private organization to serve as a central hub for internal phone communication and as a proxy for communication with outer world, it is usually called a Private Branch Exchange (PBX). These PBXs usually operate with both VoIP as well as classic telephone networks (PSTN), acting as gateways between those two technologies. The following text focuses on misuse of such gateways.

3.2   Principle of the Fraud

Depending on configuration a PBX may allow users to make VoIP calls to PSTN numbers by setting the destination user ID in an INVITE request to the called number prepended by a special prefix. For example, to call a PSTN number 555-555-0123 a SIP call to 995555550123@example.com needs to be performed, assuming that the gateway is located at example.com and it has "99" configured as the prefix for PSTN calls.

The attack is based on finding poorly secured PBXs and using them to make fraudulent calls to PSTN. Motivations to make such calls may differ, but the common one is to gain money by calling to paid services. This is outlined in Fig. 1. The attacker first loans a premium-rate phone number[1], usually in a foreign country and via some intermediary company. Any calls to that number generate revenue for the attacker. Computers controlled by the attacker are then instructed to find open PBXs and make fake calls via them. When a call is

---

[1] *I. e.* a number which is charged at a high rate in favour of the line operator.

mention brute-force attacks against authentication mechanism, which are somewhat similar to the prefix-guessing attacks described in this paper. They however do not present any countermeasures or a way of detection of such attacks.

Another work enumerating possible attacks against VoIP technology is a survey by A. Keromytis [12]. Although it summarizes hundreds of papers from the area, there is no mention about the kind of attack we deal with, nor any work using flow measurement to detect security threats in VoIP traffic.

To our best knowledge, the only paper providing a way of detection of toll fraud attempts is [8] by Hoffstadt et al. It is focused on monitoring of VoIP threats using honeypots. The authors describe principle of toll fraud based on hijacking of a SIP account. An attacker that gains a user's identity is able to establish a phone call that can be charged. Discovery of a fraud is based on an off-line analysis of honeypot logs. Even though the authors stated that they observed manual attempts of toll fraud, we are observing automatic brute-force guesses of dialing prefixes. Also, our flow-based approach allows to monitor traffic going to real gateways, not only honeypots, therefore we are able to detect real attacks and possibly raise alerts on the successful ones.

Besides common hardware and software VoIP phones, there are several tools that allow users to communicate over SIP in unusual ways. For example, they allow to craft a request with any values of headers or to perform brute-force attacks automatically. Examples of the tools are [6,11,13,15].

A detailed description of the flow monitoring technology can be found in the article [9] by Hofstede et al. It also contains an overview of available software. The paper [14] by Velan and Celeda introduces the concept of application-aware flow monitoring.

3   Principle of the Phone Call Fraud

The following subsection provides a brief introduction to VoIP telephony and SIP. We focus only on aspects needed to understand the type of fraud discussed in this paper and the proposed detection method; we knowingly leave out many otherwise important details for brevity.

3.1   Short Introduction to SIP

Voice over IP is a technology for transferring voice and multimedial data over computer networks. Session Initiation Protocol (SIP) is the well-known protocol used for initiation, control and termination of VoIP sessions (or calls). The multimedial data are transferred in a separate channel using Real-time Transport Protocol (RTP).

SIP is a protocol based on a request-response transaction model. Every device can act both as a client or as a server. The client creates and sends requests, the server receives and processes them, and generates one or more replies. The high-level architecture consists mostly of end devices (hardware or software phones) and SIP proxy servers. The proxies receive requests for calls, localize called parties and route the requests to them (possibly via other proxies). They also route

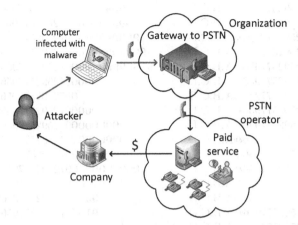

Fig. 1. Principle of the SIP fraud

successful, the PSTN operator charges the organization operating the PBX. The money goes to the company operating the premium line and to the attacker.

In order to make calls to PSTN via a PBX, the attacker needs to know the prefix which must be prepended in front of the number. Since this prefix depends on a particular PBX and its configuration, attackers usually do not know it. They must therefore guess it by trying various possibilities until the correct prefix is found and the call is successful or until all possibilities from a dictionary are used and the attacker moves on to another victim.

Such guessing can be recognized as a large number of INVITE requests from the same source, all trying to call the same number but with different prefixes. A typical sequence of URIs in the INVITE requests is shown in Fig. 2.

Such a sequence typically contains tens of INVITE requests with different prefixes. All the prefixes may be tried within a few minutes, but attackers often try to evade detection by putting long intervals between individual trials, so it may take up to several days. Such slow attacks are harder to notice in logs and generally harder to detect by any means.

In some cases, PBXs are configured insecurely and allow to make such calls without a proper authentication. More secured PBXs require an authentication header in the INVITE request. In such a case, attackers can perform a dictionary attack first, in order to find login credentials of some user. If some login and password is successfully found, the attacker may impersonate the user and the prefix guessing can be run in the same way as described. This paper focuses solely on the prefix guessing part of attacks. The detection method described in the next section makes no difference between authenticated and non-authenticated users.

4 Detection Method

The detection method is designed to work without any prior knowledge of VoIP infrastructure and dialing plans on the network. The assumed deployment is on

00972592577956@A.B.C.D	9999990972592577956@A.B.C.D
000972592577956@A.B.C.D	99999990972592577956@A.B.C.D
900972592577956@A.B.C.D	999999990972592577956@A.B.C.D
+972592577956@A.B.C.D	9999999990972592577956@A.B.C.D
972592577956@A.B.C.D	99999999990972592577956@A.B.C.D
100972592577956@A.B.C.D	9000972592577956@A.B.C.D
800972592577956@A.B.C.D	0972592577956@A.B.C.D
600972592577956@A.B.C.D	0000972592577956@A.B.C.D
700972592577956@A.B.C.D	0000000972592577956@A.B.C.D
400972592577956@A.B.C.D	00000000972592577956@A.B.C.D
300972592577956@A.B.C.D	000000000972592577956@A.B.C.D
200972592577956@A.B.C.D	0000000000972592577956@A.B.C.D
500972592577956@A.B.C.D	91000972592577956@A.B.C.D
99900972592577956@A.B.C.D	9900972592577956@A.B.C.D
999900972592577956@A.B.C.D	9100972592577956@A.B.C.D
9999900972592577956@A.B.C.D	. . .

Fig. 2. An example of URIs called during a typical prefix guessing attack (IP address anonymized)

an ISP level or in a network of a large organization, where an operator of the detection system has no direct control over VoIP equipment but still wants to know about any issues related to it.

The detection is based on an analysis of SIP INVITE requests trying to make calls to PSTN numbers. The goal is to find IP addresses that generate large number of such requests varying only in a prefix of the called number. The detection method works even if prefixes are tried in a very low rate (e.g. one attempt per day). Also, it was needed to design the method to be efficient since we are targeting large networks with high volumes of traffic.

The input data comes from flow monitoring probes. Basic flow records are not sufficient for the detection of the SIP fraud, it is needed to extract additional information from SIP headers. In particular, we extended the flow records by *request/response code*, *Request-URI* and *To*, *From*, *Call-ID* and *User-Agent* headers from SIP messages. We achieved this by using a plugin for FlowMon probes [10]. It is the probe able to monitor high speed networks and parse information from application layer protocols. The whole monitoring infrastructure is shown in Fig. 3. Data from the monitoring probes are passed to a collector in the IPFIX format [3] and then into the Nemea system [1,2] – a modular framework for network traffic analysis and anomaly detection. The detection method described in the following paragraphs was implemented as a software module for the Nemea system. It receives and analyses extended flow records of SIP traffic and reports detected attacks.

The detection algorithm works as follows. For each incoming flow record carrying information about an INVITE request a called party identification is taken from *Request-URI* (or *To* header, depending on configuration; however, both are usually the same). If its *user* part, i.e. the part before the @, contains only digits or some of the allowed special symbols (+, *, #, -, :) it is further processed. Otherwise, the message is ignored since it is not a call to a phone number.

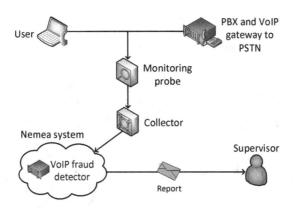

Fig. 3. Infrastructure of the monitoring system with the detection module

Responses to the INVITE messages are also processed and are used for determination whether the call was successfully established. In particular, when an OK response is observed after a previous INVITE request and their *Call-ID* headers match, the call is considered to be successful.

A set of URIs observed in INVITE requests is stored for each source IP address. In order to allow efficient storage and analysis of such sets, the URIs are stored into a specially designed data structure based on the suffix tree. Figure 4 shows an example of a set of URIs stored in such a tree. In the suffix tree, the common suffix of two or more URIs is represented by a parent node while the children nodes (or subtrees) represent their different prefixes. There is a rule that none of nodes can have a common part with its sibling. Therefore, in case a newly inserted URI contains an unknown prefix which has a common part with some existing prefix, it can cause a split of an existing node.

Each node represents an URI given by its value concatenated with values of all its ascendants. Each node also contains a number of call attempts to that URI, number of successfully established calls and other information, mostly for optimization of the detection algorithm.

Such a tree is constructed for each source IP address and is continuously updated as new INVITE requests from that address are observed. The trees are periodically analyzed in order to detect prefix guessing attacks. As shown in Sec. 3.2, during such attack a large number of URIs is observed with the same phone number and destination host but many different prefixes. That results in a tree in which there is a single node which contains the phone number and have a large number of descendants.

The algorithm for detection of such a node works with two parameters – maximal prefix length (l_{max}) and a threshold on number of tested unique prefixes (T). At first, the tree is traversed from the bottom to the top (i.e. from leaves to the root). For each leaf node, the algorithm goes up through its ascendants until the total length of numbers stored in the visited nodes exceeds l_{max}. The final node potentially represents the called number. Then, the number of its descen-

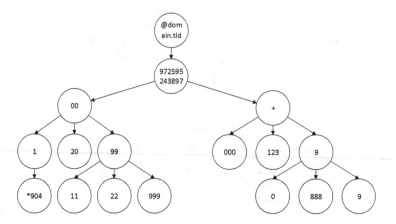

Fig. 4. Suffix tree for analysis of phone number prefixes

dants satisfying the following two conditions is counted: 1) the prefix represented by a node must be shorter than l_{max} and 2) there must be an unsuccessful call attempt made to the node's URI. If the number of such descendants is the same or higher than the threshold T, an attack is reported. Otherwise, the algorithm continues traversing the tree from another leaf node.

After the attack is reported, all related nodes are removed from the tree, so the same attack is not reported in the next run of the algorithm. Basic information about the attack is however kept. Therefore, if the attack continues by trying another prefixes and their number again exceeds the threshold, so it is detected as an attack, it is recognized that it is only a continuation of the attack reported earlier. The new detection is thus reported only as an update of the previous one.

Besides the suffix tree, some other information is stored per IP address, mostly for the purpose of reporting. This information includes the time of the last seen SIP message, the time of the last detected attack or the value of the *User-Agent* header.

The detector is designed for continuous processing of potentially infinite stream of data from the network. Some of the incoming data are stored in memory, but because the capacity of available memory is always limited, old data must be periodically removed. Most of the data removals are based on a simple timeout. If no SIP communication from an IP address has been detected for a given time period, all information about that address is removed. The default timeout in our implementation is 14 days. Also, if a suffix tree of some address grows into a huge size (we use a threshold of 100,000 nodes), the whole tree is removed. Because such a big tree is often the result of a large attack, the detection algorithm is applied to the tree before removal. Finally, nodes representing prefixes in an attack are removed after the attack is reported, as was described earlier.

5   Evaluation

In order to evaluate the detection method, we prepared a SIP server simulating a PBX with a gateway to PSTN. The server was configured to not require authentication and to allow calls to PSTN using a three-digit prefix. A modified SIPVicious tool [6] (svwar.py script) was used to generate attacks to the server from several sources. The simulated attackers tried to call to a number with randomly changing prefixes until they guessed the correct one. The traffic between the attacking machines and the server was monitored by the detector. Both parameters of the detection algorithm, that is the maximal length of a prefix (l_{max}) and the minimal number of call attempts that is considered as a guessing (T), were set to 10.

At first, the tests were performed in a virtual environment with no other traffic than the generated attacks. As expected, all attacks were successfully detected and reported, except a few cases in which the correct prefix was guessed in less than 10 tries (such attacks could be detected as well by decreasing the threshold T, but too low threshold might cause false alerts when deployed on real network).

We continued by tests in the real environment – in the CESNET2 network. CESNET2 is the academic network of the Czech Republic, connecting Czech universities and many other organizations to the Internet (around 1 million IP addresses in total). Its perimeter – 10 peering links, all with wire speed of 10 Gbps – is monitored using FlowMon probes. The total traffic on these links ranges from 5 Gb/s at night to 25 Gb/s during the day (50k to 150k flow records per second). The average amount of SIP traffic is around 50 flows per second, with occasional peaks up to several hundreds.

The probes were running the plugin for extending flow records with values of SIP headers. The detector was deployed into an operational instance of the Nemea system which receives and analyzes flow records from all the probes. The SIP server and the machine simulating attacks were placed so that the traffic between them is observed by one of the monitoring probes. Configuration of the server, attacks and the detector was the same as before.

Despite the generated attacks were hidden in a lot of real traffic now, all the attacks consisting of at least 10 attempts were successfully detected again, no matter how slow or fast they were. A lot of real attacks were detected, too.

In a measurement period of two weeks, the detector received and analyzed 10.5 million flow records corresponding to SIP INVITE messages. There were 15,992 prefix guessing attacks reported consisting of 201,438 INVITE messages. That means that on average 12.6 prefixes are tried by a single attacker at a single gateway. Around 1.9 % of all INVITE messages were marked as part of this kind of attacks (although we expect that many of the others are malicious as well, since authentication attacks generate a lot of INVITE messages, too). Approximately 1.1 % of attacks seemed to be successful[2], i.e. a call was successfully established.

---

[2] Not every successful attempt necessarily means a breach of a real gateway. Some of the gateways may in fact be honeypots.

Table 1. Top-20 prefixes observed in the backbone network traffic

Prefix	Count	Succ. calls	Prefix	Count	Succ. calls
00	3800	22	9	1946	2
000	3412	9	810	1706	6
900	3273	12	9000	1608	8
+	3072	13	9900	1599	4
(none)	2498	8	9011	1582	7
0000	2464	14	99900	1462	10
011	2286	3	9009	1330	2
800	2248	5	9810	1323	9
0011	2092	4	005	1303	2
009	1982	5	001	1297	8

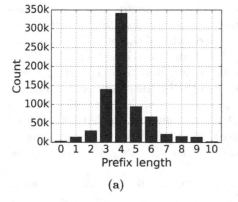

(a)

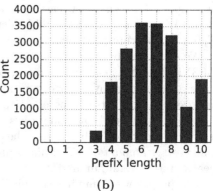

(b)

Fig. 5. Histogram of the lengths of a) all prefixes tried in attacks, b) the longest prefixes tried in attacks

During its operation, the detection module consumed about 200 MB of memory and took only about 5 % of CPU on average (Intel(R) Xeon(R) CPU E5-2630 @ 2.30 GHz).

During our testing of the detection module, we gathered a lot of information and statistics about the SIP attacks as well as the SIP traffic in general. The interesting results are summarized in the rest of this section.

Table 1 shows a list of the 20 most often observed prefixes that were tested by attackers. The data for the table was taken from a two week period. The "Count" column represents the number of times the prefix was used and the "Succ. calls" represents the number of successful calls that were observed with the prefix.

Figure 5a shows the histogram of lengths of all prefixes that were used in attacks reported within a two week period. Figure 5b shows the histogram of the longest prefixes that were used in the reported attacks. That means it shows the maximal length of prefixes used in individual attacks. It can be observed

Table 2. The most frequent values of the *User-Agent* header

User-Agent	Count
sipcli/v1.8	643,312
friendly-scanner	424,178
Cisco-SIPGateway/IOS-12.x	6,304
FPBX-2.10.1(1.8.7.1	1,153
Asterisk PBX 11.11.0	570
None or empty	2,440
Other values	7,220

that while most prefixes have 3 or 4 digits, attacks almost always contain some longer prefixes as well.

Table 2 shows the most frequent values of the *User-Agent* header that were observed on the backbone network. The data for the table was taken from a one week interval. There were 384 distinct values of the header. As can be seen, the most often used user agents (*sipcli, friendly-scanner*[3]) are scripts that allow users/attackers to craft SIP messages with any values of headers. They can be used to generate e.g. phone numbers of the callee in the case of prefix guessing. Of course, the *User-Agent* header cannot be a reliable source of information since a client can fill in any string. However, a legitimate client usually does not have any reason to present itself by the name of another tool and malicious clients apparently do not do that often.

6   Conclusion

This paper presented a possible usage of the emerging technology of application-aware flow monitoring in the area of security threat detection. In particular, a method for detection of VoIP-based toll fraud – a network attack that can lead to a significant financial losses – has been proposed. The detection is enabled by special flow monitoring probes which are able to extend flow records by information from application-layer protocols.

Using exported headers of Session Initiation Protocol (SIP), the proposed detection module is able to analyze SIP transactions and detect attempts to guess a prefix configured on a PBX to allow calls to PSTN. It is also able to detect whether any of the attempts was successful. A successful call after a previous guessing indicates that the attacker found a way to make unauthorized calls via the PBX. In such a case it is necessary to alert an operator of the PBX immediately.

An implementation of the method was deployed and evaluated on a real backbone network. Some interesting results of the SIP analysis in real network traffic were presented in Sec. 5. The information from the extended flow records allows us to observe statistics about *User-Agent* headers and called phone numbers,

---

[3] *friendly-scanner* is the default *User-Agent* value used by SIPVicious tool.

for example. The detection capabilities of the proposed method are very good according to our experiments – all simulated attacks were successfully detected, as well as many real attacks. In fact, any attack consisting of at least 10 `INVITE` requests in a time window of 14 days is detected in default configuration. Of course, these thresholds can be tuned to fit requirements of the network operators.

While these attacks may be detected by other methods as well, for example by analysing logs of SIP servers, the flow monitoring approach allows to monitor all SIP servers in the network from one place, without necessity of access to the servers (which are usually operated by other people than those responsible for security). Moreover, if the detector is deployed on backbone links, like in our test scenario, it allows to observe attacks from many different sources to many different destinations, which is impossible with other methods (log parsing or honeypots). It provides us with more complete view on attacks and attackers. For example, by deep analysis of attack characteristics and their sources, it may be possible to detect groups of IP addresses attacking collectively, which can lead to revealing botnets.

Acknowledgments. This work was partially supported by the "CESNET Large Infrastructure" (LM2010005), CTU grant No. SGS15/122/OHK3/1T/18 funded by the Ministry of Education, Youth and Sports of the Czech Republic, and BUT grant FIT-S-14-2297. This work was also supported by the IT4Innovations Centre of Excellence project (CZ.1.05/1.1.00/02.0070), funded by the European Regional Development Fund and the national budget of the Czech Republic via the Research and Development for Innovations Operational Programme, as well as Czech Ministry of Education, Youth and Sports via the project Large Research, Development and Innovations Infrastructures (LM2011033).

References

1. Bartos, V., Zadnik, M., Cejka, T.: Nemea: Framework for stream-wise analysis of network traffic. Tech. rep., CESNET (2013)
2. CESNET: Nemea, https://www.liberouter.org/nemea/
3. Claise, B., et al.: Specification of the IP Flow Information Export (IPFIX) Protocol for the Exchange of Flow Information. RFC 7011 (September 2013)
4. Communications Fraud Control Association: 2013 CFCA Global Fraud Loss Survey. Press release (October 2013), http://www.cfca.org/pdf/survey/CFCA2013GlobalFraudLossSurvey-pressrelease.pdf
5. El-moussa, F., Mudhar, P., Jones, A.: Overview of SIP attacks and countermeasures. In: Weerasinghe, D. (ed.) ISDF 2009. LNICST, vol. 41, pp. 82–91. Springer, Heidelberg (2010)
6. Gauci, S.: SIPVicious. Tools for auditing sip based voip systems (2012), https://code.google.com/p/sipvicious/
7. Hellemons, L., Hendriks, L., Hofstede, R., Sperotto, A., Sadre, R., Pras, A.: SSHCure: A Flow-Based SSH Intrusion Detection System. In: Sadre, R., Novotný, J., Čeleda, P., Waldburger, M., Stiller, B. (eds.) AIMS 2012. LNCS, vol. 7279, pp. 86–97. Springer, Heidelberg (2012)

8. Hoffstadt, D., Marold, A., Rathgeb, E.: Analysis of SIP-Based Threats Using a VoIP Honeynet System. In: Proccedings of the 11th International Conference on Trust, Security and Privacy in Computing and Communications (TrustCom), pp. 541–548 (June 2012)
9. Hofstede, R., Celeda, P., Trammell, B., Drago, I., Sadre, R., Sperotto, A., Pras, A.: Flow monitoring explained: From packet capture to data analysis with netflow and ipfix. IEEE Communications Surveys Tutorials 16(4), 2037–2064 (2014)
10. INVEA-TECH a.s.: FlowMon Probe – High-performance NetFlow Probe up to 10 Gbps, http://www.invea-tech.com/products-and-services/flowmon/flowmon -probes
11. KaplanSoft: SipCLI, http://www.kaplansoft.com/sipcli/
12. Keromytis, A.D.: A comprehensive survey of voice over ip security research. IEEE Communications Surveys & Tutorials 14(2), 514–537 (2012)
13. Ohlmeier, N.: SIP Swiss Army Knife (Sipsak), http://sourceforge.net/projects/sipsak.berlios/
14. Velan, P., Čeleda, P.: Next generation application-aware flow monitoring. In: Sperotto, A., Doyen, G., Latré, S., Charalambides, M., Stiller, B. (eds.) AIMS 2014. LNCS, vol. 8508, pp. 173–178. Springer, Heidelberg (2014)
15. VoP Security: SiVuS (SiP Vulnerability Scanner) – User Guide v1.07, http://www.voip-security.net/pdfs/SiVuS-User-Doc1.7.pdf

Schengen Routing: A Compliance Analysis

Daniel Dönni[✉], Guilherme Sperb Machado,
Christos Tsiaras, and Burkhard Stiller

University of Zurich, Department of Informatics,
Binzmühlestrasse 14, CH-8050 Zurich, Switzerland
{doenni,machado,tsiaras,stiller}@ifi.uzh.ch

Abstract. Schengen Routing was proposed as a countermeasure to traffic monitoring activities practiced by intelligence agencies. This work here presents the results of a larger-scale measurement performed to quantify Schengen Routing compliance in today's Internet. Based on 3388 TCP, UDP, and ICMP traceroute measurements executed from RIPE Atlas probes located in over 1100 different Autonomous Systems (AS) in the Schengen Area, it was found that 34.5% to 39.7% of these routes are Schengen-compliant, while compliance levels vary from 0% to 80% among countries. Finally, an approach was developed that allows end-users to determine whether a specific route to a host is Schengen-compliant or not.

Keywords: Schengen Routing · Geo-location · Compliance checks

1 Introduction

The affair involving Edward Snowden and the National Security Agency (NSA) in 2013 demonstrated that wiretapping large amounts of Internet traffic data was not only possible, but also applied on a regular basis by various intelligence agencies in violation of privacy laws [13]. However, the controversy only came into broader political debate by the time it was alleged that several European state heads had become victims of the wiretapping activities themselves [2].

In the context of the political and technical debate that followed, the idea of *Schengen Routing* demonstrated to be a possible amendment to protect communications across Europe. The term *Schengen* refers to the treaty targeted at reducing border controls and implementing a harmonized legal framework [9]. Those countries, who signed the Schengen Treaty, form the Schengen Area. Table 1 shows the current Schengen members. It is important to highlight that the Schengen Area is not equivalent to the European Union (EU), since some countries belonging to the EU are not part of Schengen (*e.g.*, United Kingdom), while Schengen also comprises non-EU countries (*e.g.*, Switzerland).

Schengen Routing refers to the practice of routing Internet traffic between hosts located in the Schengen Area, not leaving the borders of countries part of the Schengen Treaty. Such Internet traffic not leaving the Schengen Area is more difficult to be wiretapped by non-Schengen intelligence agencies, since the Internet traffic remains still unencrypted. However, this traffic remains still vulnerable to wiretapping activities that may occur within Schengen [16].

© IFIP International Federation for Information Processing 2015
S. Latré et al. (Eds.): AIMS 2015, LNCS 9122, pp. 100–112, 2015.
DOI: 10.1007/978-3-319-20034-7_11

Table 1. Schengen members as of January 2015

Country Code	Country Name	Country Code	Country Name
AT	Austria	IT	Italy
BE	Belgium	LI	Liechtenstein
CH	Switzerland	LT	Lithuania
CZ	Czech Republic	LU	Luxemburg
DE	Germany	LV	Latvia
DK	Denmark	MT	Malta
EE	Estonia	NL	Netherlands
ES	Spain	NO	Norway
FI	Finland	PL	Poland
FR	France	PT	Portugal
GR	Greece	SE	Sweden
HU	Hungary	SI	Slovenia
IS	Island	SK	Slovakia

An implementation of Schengen routing requires the reconfiguration of routing tables and the renegotiation of transit and peering agreements. The effort required depends significantly on the degree to which current routing already complies with Schengen routing or not. However, there is no previous work available, which measured a Schengen routing compliance through active measurements by analyzing TCP, ICMP, and UDP traffic. Thus, this paper answers the following question: What is the Schengen routing compliance or non-compliance percentage of current traffic among Schengen countries based on the observation of active measurements?

For that a large number of traceroute measurements was executed by applying RIPE Atlas [17] probes located in Autonomous Systems (AS) within Schengen to a well-known host in Switzerland, being part of the Schengen Area. ASes were chosen as the unit of analysis, because ASes are collections of network devices managed by a single administrative authority that can decide to cooperate with government agencies or not. IP addresses of nodes along a network path can be determined by using the traceroute tool. By means of a database, such as GeoLite [10], IP addresses obtained can be related to ASes and countries and, thus, placed in- or outside Schengen. Next to these measurements, a tool termed chkroute has been developed, allowing end-users to find out whether specific routes are Schengen-compliant.

This paper is structured as follows. Section 2 presents related work. The approach applied and evaluations performed are described in Sections 3 and 4, respectively. Section 5 presents the chkroute tool developed. Finally, Section 6 summarizes the work, draws conclusions, and outlines future steps.

2   Related Work

The most detailed work analyzing routes leaving the Schengen Area was performed by [16]. Publically accessible BGP routing tables were obtained and, based on BGP routing entries, a graph of ASes was generated. Based on these graphs, traffic routes were established and analyzed to assess whether traffic between two peers within the Schengen Area would leave the area, thus, pointing on non-compliant Schengen Area routes. It was assumed that an AS belongs to a particular country, if the majority of its allocated Internet Protocol (IP) address space is bound to that country. Therefore, if an AS hosts IP addresses used in countries X, Y, and Z, but more than 50% is allocated to country X, the AS is considered to be located in country X. Such an assumption simplifies the full process of binding ASes to particular countries. However, it may present non-realistic results, since some ASes can present logical connections to several countries that not necessarily reflect the true country of origin of such an AS [19]. Those results show that, *e.g.*, in Belgium, Switzerland, and Spain, more than one third of available routes are operating via ASes located outside the respective country. It is further found that the number of routes leaving the Schengen Area substantially varies among countries, *e.g.*, 0% in Iceland and 35.38% in Belgium.

Another approach analyzed the content of BGP routing tables [12]. The respective outcomes are beneficial due to 3 reasons:

1. BGP looking glasses are servers running specific software designed to retrieve routing information. These servers are found in a considerable number of strategic ASes around the globe.
2. Evaluating BGP routing tables is a passive and, thus, less intrusive approach to form an AS graph.
3. BGP routing tables present a wider view of routing possibilities within each AS.

The major disadvantage of this approach is the lack of certainty that a packet will follow the inferred AS graph to a specific destination as the information may be incomplete or out of date.

Therefore, active measurements involving tools such as, *e.g.*, traceroute, are employed to discover Internet routes that are being used in practice for particular protocols and traffic [3]. Moreover, traceroute measurements are able to (1) reveal multiple routers within an AS and not only an AS-level graph representation, and (2) provide a real time result of the current network hops from source to destination. Thus, Paris traceroute [1] provides a more realistic routing map compared to the classic traceroute tool, solving problems caused by the current vast deployment of load balancers in the Internet. Paris traceroute addresses per-flow load balancers, varying header fields, such as the TCP/ICMP sequence number, the UDP checksum, and the ICMP identifier. The chkroute tool uses Paris traceroute to collect routing information (*i.e.*, IP addresses of network hops) from the source to the destination, and uses the GeoLite database [10] to map IP address ranges to ASes. Table 2 summarizes major characteristics of chkroute and [16] to analyze Schengen Routing compliance.

A major disadvantage of Schengen routing is that Internet traffic remains unencrypted. As a consequence, it is still vulnerable to wiretapping activities from within Schengen. A wide-spread use of end-to-end encryption would resolve this issue [16].

Table 2. Characteristics comparison of approaches analyzing Schengen Routing compliance

	Characteristics			
Approaches	Based on Active Measurements	Based on Passive Measurements	Uses GeoLite Database	Provide Compliance in Real Time
[16]	no	yes	yes	no
chkroute	no	yes	yes	yes

3 Approach

To measure Schengen routing compliance, a larger-scale measurement has been performed. RIPE Atlas [17] was chosen as a measurement platform due to its high AS coverage. ASes were selected for anlysis, because they appear as units controlled by a single administrative entity defining routing policies that has the capability to coopreate with intelligence agencies or not.

3.1 Test-Bed Selection

To perform real-life measurements at a larger scale, a suitable test-bed is needed. Test-beds had to meet two requirements to be taken into consideration:

1. The test-bed had to be able to run traceroute measurements to retrieve IP addresses of nodes along a routing path.
2. The test-bed had to provide a high AS coverage in the Schengen Area.

Several test-beds could have been used to perform larger-scale measurements: Planet-Lab [15], EMANICSLab [8], Bismark [18], and RIPE Atlas [17].

On one hand, Planet-Lab [15] and EMANICSLab [8] provide administrative access to the machines and, therefore, allow for full control over all aspects of the experiment. On the other hand, the number of ASes currently covered by these test-beds in Europe is lower when compared to RIPE Atlas: EMANICSLab provide nodes in 11 different ASes, while Planet-Lab provides nodes in 69 ASes. In contrast, RIPE Atlas provides 1306 ASes in the Schengen Area alone. Since Planet-Lab and EMANICSLab nodes are predominantly located in academic and research networks, such a distribution may not necessarily be representative for assessing Schengen routing compliance in the Schengen Internet as a whole [7].

The project Bismark [18] allows researchers to perform measurements from home routers equipped with a modified openWRT firmware [14]. The project cannot be used to study Schengen compliance, since there are only 178 routers globally available, and even less within Schengen as of 2014 [18].

RIPE Atlas is a measurement infrastructure initiated and coordinated by RIPE NCC [17]. According to RIPE's website, "RIPE NCC is building the largest measurement infrastructure ever made" [17]. The RIPE Atlas measurement infrastructure is based on a large number of low-cost measurement nodes given away for free to volunteers willing to host those probes in their private, institutional, or public networks. In exchange for hosting a probe, volunteers get access to measurement statistics and obtain credits that can be traded for running user-defined measurements on the infrastructure. The RIPE Atlas measurement infrastructure provides the best AS coverage by a substantial margin (1306 different ASes in Schengen alone) and was, therefore, chosen for the Schengen routing compliance analysis.

3.2 AS Selection

To determine to what extent traffic complies with Schengen Routing, a list of ASes in the Schengen Area had to be selected. Maxmind provides a free geolocation database named GeoLite [10], which maps IP address ranges to ASes and countries. The respective information is provided in two separate files. The first file contains IP address ranges in a long representation along with an AS number (*e.g.,* 5 10 AS1). The second file contains IP address ranges in a long representation along with a country code (*e.g.,* 5 10 CH). Based on this information, the number of IP addresses per AS and country was calculated (*e.g.,* AS1 has 10 - 5 + 1 = 6 IP addresses in CH (Switzerland)). These AS and country ranges did not always match and had to be divided into matching subranges in these cases. The logic for calculating the number of IP addresses per country remained the same. ASes were included in the measurement effort, if they had at least one IP address in a Schengen country. The resulting number of ASes in the Schengen Area was 9967 (*cf.* Table 3).

Table 3. Number of ASes after results processing (T: TCP, U: UDP, I: ICMP)

Original	Not Covered	No Probes			Failed/Error			Outside Schengen			Remaining		
		T	U	I	T	U	I	T	U	I	T	U	I
9967	8661	44	47	50	25	24	25	105	104	106	1132	1131	1125

3.3 Measurement Execution

All traceroute measurements were executed using the RIPE Atlas measurement infrastructure. RIPE Atlas allows to specify an AS number as a measurement source and selects a suitable probe with an IP address within the AS automatically. The target IP address of all traceroute measurements was a machine located within Schengen at the premises of University of Zurich, Switzerland (within AS 559). Measurement requests were submitted for all 9967 ASes determined in Section 3.2 for the ICMP, TCP, and UDP protocol in turn. For each protocol, RIPE Atlas performed three traceroute measurements automatically.

These measurements were limited to one target host and three traceroute measurements per protocol because the number of measurements that can be performed on RIPE Atlas is limited by the credit earned by the respective volunteer.

3.4 Results Processing

All results obtained from these measurements were processed in several steps (see Table 3).

1. Measurement requests were submitted for 9967 ASes, out of which 8661 ASes were not covered by RIPE Atlas. They could, therefore, not be taken into consideration.
2. RIPE Atlas could not find suitable probing devices in all ASes covered. These ASes could not be taken into consideration.
3. Some measurements failed or produced invalid results (*e.g.*, error messages rather than measurement data) and were excluded.
4. ASes may have IP address ranges advertised in several countries, especially in ASes with large number of IP address subnets. Because RIPE Atlas chooses IP addresses within the AS at its discrection, an IP address outside the Schengen Area may be selected. Measurements executed from probes having IP addresses located outside the Schengen Area were excluded.

After this results processing, 1132 TCP, 1131 UDP, and 1125 ICMP valid measurements remained for an evaluation. The unprocessed traceroute files obtained from RIPE Atlas measurements have been made publically available [5].

4 Evaluation

These results obtained were classified with respect to Schengen routing compliance as follows:

1. Measurements containing at least one IP address located outside the Schengen Area were classified as "Non-compliant" (NC).
2. Measurements containing only IP addresses inside the Schengen Area were classified as "Compliant" (C).
3. Measurements containing IP addresses for which no country information was available or for which traceroute did not produce an IP address were classified as "Unknown" (U), if all other IP addresses were located within Schengen and "Non-Compliant" otherwise

To determine the geographic location of an IP address, Maxmind's GeoLite database [10] was used, the same database as was used for the AS selection process described in Section 3.2. Figure 1 provides an overview of those results found. Light gray shades represent higher Schengen routing compliance levels while dark gray shades stand for lower compliance levels.

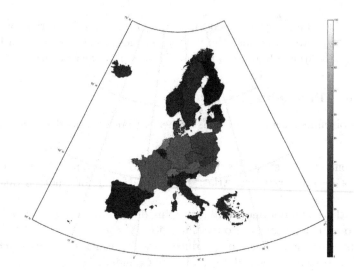

Fig. 1. Schengen routing compliance levels

All detailed results are shown in Table 4. The "R" column ranks the Schengen countries – represented by their ISO code – according to the relative amount of compliant TCP routes. TCP was chosen for ranking, since it is the most frequently used transport protocol in the Internet as of today. The "ASes" column represents the number of ASes for which traceroute measurements have been performed. "T" represents the total number of measurements that were performed for the respective country and protocol. "C", "NC", and "U" show the amount of routes that were compliant, non-compliant, and unknown, respectively. For each of these categories the absolute and relative values are provided.

4.1 Results Analysis

This section discusses the results presented in Table 4, providing insight into compliant, non-compliant, and unknown routes.

Overall compliance levels range from 34.5% in the TCP case, to 37.4% in the UDP, and 39.7% in the ICMP case. The variation among countries is substantial, though, it ranges from 0% (TCP), 0% (UDP) and 0% (ICMP) in the case of Malta (MT) to 80% (TCP), 75% (UDP), and 80% (ICMP) in the case of Liechtenstein (LI). These results show that no country is fully compliant with Schengen routing for those active measurement results.

Overall non-compliance levels range from 33.8% in the TCP case to 38.7% in the UDP and 42.3% in the ICMP case. As it happens for the compliance level, the variation among countries is considerable, it ranges from 0% (TCP) and 20% (ICMP) in the case of Liechtenstein (LI) and 19.4% (UDP) in the case of Switzerland (CH) to 81.8% (TCP), 81.8% (UDP), and 84.8% (ICMP) in the case of Estonia (EE).

The relative amount of unknown routes ranges from 31.7% in the TCP case to 23.9% in the UDP and 17.9% in the ICMP case. The variation among countries is

Table 4. Schengen Routing compliance analysis

R	ISO	TCP ASes	T	C	C (%)	NC	NC (%)	U	U (%)	UDP ASes	T	C	C (%)	NC	NC (%)	U	U (%)	ICMP ASes	T	C	C (%)	NC	NC (%)	U	U (%)
1	LI	5	15	12	80.0%	0	0.0%	3	20.0%	4	12	9	75.0%	3	25.0%	0	0.0%	5	15	12	80.0%	3	20.0%	0	0.0%
2	NL	88	264	148	56.1%	51	19.3%	65	24.6%	88	264	165	62.5%	65	24.6%	34	12.9%	88	264	161	61.0%	68	25.8%	35	13.3%
3	CH	66	198	102	51.5%	30	15.2%	66	33.3%	67	201	126	62.7%	39	19.4%	36	17.9%	66	198	132	66.7%	44	22.2%	22	11.1%
4	AT	56	168	79	47.0%	42	25.0%	47	28.0%	56	168	77	45.8%	59	35.1%	32	19.0%	56	168	89	53.0%	64	38.1%	15	8.9%
5	DE	192	576	253	43.9%	187	32.5%	136	23.6%	189	567	266	46.9%	198	34.9%	103	18.2%	188	564	280	49.6%	210	37.2%	74	13.1%
6	FR	115	345	143	41.4%	91	26.4%	111	32.2%	117	351	155	44.2%	94	26.8%	102	29.1%	114	342	170	49.7%	111	32.5%	61	17.8%
7	HU	20	60	24	40.0%	23	38.3%	13	21.7%	21	63	28	44.4%	26	41.3%	9	14.3%	20	60	27	45.0%	27	45.0%	6	10.0%
8	CZ	81	243	90	37.0%	76	31.3%	77	31.7%	80	240	91	37.9%	83	34.6%	66	27.5%	81	243	102	42.0%	94	38.7%	47	19.3%
9	DK	38	114	42	36.8%	30	26.3%	42	36.8%	38	114	53	46.5%	33	28.9%	28	24.6%	38	114	53	46.5%	36	31.6%	25	21.9%
10	LT	11	33	12	36.4%	12	36.4%	9	27.3%	11	33	13	39.4%	11	33.3%	9	27.3%	11	33	13	39.4%	12	36.4%	8	24.2%
11	PL	78	234	81	34.6%	96	41.0%	57	24.4%	78	234	73	31.2%	108	46.2%	53	22.6%	78	234	78	33.3%	117	50.0%	39	16.7%
12	LU	19	57	18	31.6%	27	47.4%	12	21.1%	19	57	15	26.3%	30	52.6%	12	21.1%	19	57	17	29.8%	33	57.9%	7	12.3%
13	SK	13	39	12	30.8%	13	33.3%	14	35.9%	13	39	12	30.8%	16	41.0%	11	28.2%	13	39	12	30.8%	19	48.7%	8	20.5%
14	SE	58	174	41	23.6%	53	30.5%	80	46.0%	58	174	72	41.4%	63	36.2%	39	22.4%	59	177	69	39.0%	69	39.0%	39	22.0%
15	IT	70	210	39	18.6%	66	31.4%	105	50.0%	70	210	43	20.5%	78	37.1%	89	42.4%	69	207	45	21.7%	77	37.2%	85	41.1%
16	NO	41	123	21	17.1%	51	41.5%	51	41.5%	41	123	17	13.8%	65	52.8%	41	33.3%	40	120	21	17.5%	62	51.7%	37	30.8%
17	GR	24	72	12	16.7%	44	61.1%	16	22.2%	24	72	12	16.7%	40	55.6%	20	27.8%	24	72	12	16.7%	46	63.9%	14	19.4%
	IS	6	18	3	16.7%	7	38.9%	8	44.4%	6	18	3	16.7%	9	50.0%	6	33.3%	6	18	3	16.7%	9	50.0%	6	33.3%
19	LV	13	39	6	15.4%	24	61.5%	9	23.1%	13	39	3	7.7%	29	74.4%	7	17.9%	13	39	3	7.7%	33	84.6%	3	7.7%
20	BE	27	81	12	14.8%	40	49.4%	29	35.8%	27	81	9	11.1%	52	64.2%	20	24.7%	26	78	14	17.9%	58	74.4%	6	7.7%
21	ES	43	129	12	9.3%	56	43.4%	61	47.3%	43	129	14	10.9%	73	56.6%	42	32.6%	42	126	16	12.7%	83	65.9%	27	21.4%
22	SI	16	48	4	8.3%	28	58.3%	16	33.3%	15	45	6	13.3%	35	77.8%	4	8.9%	16	48	6	12.5%	39	81.3%	3	6.3%
23	PT	13	39	2	5.1%	26	66.7%	11	28.2%	13	39	3	7.7%	28	71.8%	8	20.5%	13	39	3	7.7%	31	79.5%	5	12.8%
24	FI	25	75	3	4.0%	42	56.0%	30	40.0%	26	78	3	3.8%	45	57.7%	30	38.5%	26	78	3	3.8%	51	65.4%	24	30.8%
25	EE	11	33	0	0.0%	27	81.8%	6	18.2%	11	33	0	0.0%	27	81.8%	6	18.2%	11	33	0	0.0%	28	84.8%	5	15.2%
	MT	3	9	0	0.0%	6	66.7%	3	33.3%	3	9	0	0.0%	5	55.6%	4	44.4%	3	9	0	0.0%	5	55.6%	4	44.4%
Total		1132	3396	1171	34.5%	1148	33.8%	1077	31.7%	1131	3393	1268	37.4%	1314	38.7%	811	23.9%	1125	3375	1341	39.7%	1429	42.3%	605	17.9%

less pronounced for unknown routes compared to compliant and non-compliant routes, in the TCP case results range from 18.2% in Estonia (EE) to 50% in Italy (IT), in the UDP case they range from 0% in Liechtenstein (LI) to 42.4% in Italy (IT), and in the ICMP case results range from 0% in Liechtenstein (LI) to 41.1% in Italy (IT).

The core finding is that compliance levels vary significantly among individual countries and range from a very low to a very high compliance. As a consequence, overall values are of limited use. The second finding is that there is no significant variation among transport protocols with respect to the relative amount of compliant, non-compliant, and unknown routes.

4.2 Comparative Analysis

While the work [16] used a passive approach based on publically available BGP routing table information, countries were ranked according to a Schengen routing compliance score, which represents the relative amount of routes that do not comply with Schengen routing [16]. Although the geo-location information is taken from Maxmind's GeoLite database [10] in both cases, the comparison of both sets of results obtained are compared and shown in Table 5. The relative amount of non-compliant routes obtained using active measurements in the chkroute approach exceeds in almost all cases the amount obtained using the model based on BGP routing table data. An analysis discussing the reasons resulting in those differences found between [16] and the chkroute approach is omitted at this point, because the routing data used to produce results in [16] is not available.

5   Design and Implementation of the chkroute Tool

While those results presented are useful to obtain a general understanding of compliance levels in each of the individual Schengen countries, end-users are more interested to learn whether specific routes are compliant with Schengen Routing or not. Therefore, *chkroute* was designed and prototyped. The tool chkroute assesses whether a specific route complies to Schengen Routing or not and is available at [6].

The tool's architecture consists out of the 3 components depicted in Figure 2. The client desires to verify a route. The target host or IP address represents the endpoint of the route. The geo-location server stores location and compliance information about IP addresses. The compliance checks for routes are performed in four steps.

1. The client runs traceroute to the target host.
2. The client collects responses from hops along the path.
3. The client submits hops to the geo-location server.
4. The geo-location server analyzes these hops and sends country and compliance information back to the client, which prints the result.

A sample run of chkroute is shown in Figure 3. The chkroute command is executed from a client at University of Zurich towards a server of the University

Table 5. Non-compliant routes according [16] vs. chkroute

Country Code	Country	Pohlmann et al. [16]	chkroute
BE	Belgium	35.38%	49.4%
LI	Liechtenstein	29.41%	0.0%
CH	Switzerland	23.48%	15.2%
ES	Spain	21.27%	43.4%
LU	Luxembourg	21.15%	47.4%
FR	France	19.13%	26.4%
MT	Malta	17.86%	66.7%
FI	Finland	16.58%	56.0%
CZ	CzechRepublic	16.31%	31.3%
SE	Sweden	14.92%	30.5%
NL	Netherlands	13.07%	19.3%
DE	Germany	12.26%	32.5%
NO	Norway	10.31%	41.5%
GR	Greece	8.67%	61.1%
EE	Estonia	6.78%	81.8%
SK	Slovakia	6.25%	33.3%
LT	Lithuania	5.50%	36.4%
IT	Italy	3.70%	31.4%
AT	Austria	3.23%	25.0%
DK	Denmark	1.75%	26.3%
PL	Poland	1.43%	41.0%
PT	Portugal	1.39%	66.7%
LV	Latvia	1.34%	61.5%
SI	Slovenia	1.15%	58.3%
HU	Hungary	0.49%	38.3%
IS	Iceland	0.00%	38.9%

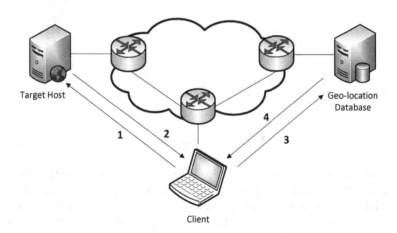

Fig. 2. The chkroute architecture

of Federal Armed Forces in Munich. Both hosts are located in Schengen. The output produces a hop count, an IP address, the country code, Schengen routing compliance information (Yes ("Y"), No ("N"), and Unknown ("Unknown")), and the AS number.

The sample output shows that this network traffic remains inside the Schengen Area until hop 7, leaves the Schengen Area for hops 8 to 11, and it returns at hop

12. Hop 13 is unknown. To ease the readability of this result, all hops are color-coded: green is for compliant, red for non-compliant, and yellow for unknown.

6   Summary, Conclusion, and Future Work

This paper presented key results of a larger-scale measurement conducted to determine the extent to which current routing is Schengen-compliant in Schengen countries. Based on 3388 TCP, UDP, and ICMP traceroute measurements run from RIPE Atlas probes located in over 1100 ASes in the Schengen Area it was found that compliance levels vary substantially among countries and range from 0% (TCP), 0% (UDP) and 0% (ICMP) in the case of Malta to 80% (TCP), 75% (UDP), and 80% (ICMP) in the case of Liechtenstein. The overall compliance levels range from 34.5% (TCP) to 37.4% (UDP) and 39.7% (ICMP).

```
daniel@daniel-csg:~/chkroute/bin$ ./chkroute.sh www.unibw.de
Hop     Host            Country         Compliant       AS No
-------------------------------------------------------------------
1       130.60.156.1    CH              Y               559
2       10.1.2.157      Local           Y               Unknown
3       10.1.0.78       Local           Y               Unknown
4       10.1.0.58       Local           Y               Unknown
5       192.41.136.65   CH              Y               559
6       192.41.136.1    CH              Y               559
7       130.59.36.1     CH              Y               559
8       62.40.124.81    GB              N               20965
9       62.40.98.76     GB              N               20965
10      62.40.98.81     GB              N               20965
11      62.40.112.146   GB              N               20965
12      188.1.144.186   DE              Y               680
13      *               Unknown         Unknown         Unknown
14      188.1.231.254   DE              Y               680
15      137.193.9.169   DE              Y               680
16      137.193.6.24    DE              Y               680
```

Fig. 3. chkroute output

Based on these measurements performed, this paper concludes that Schengen Routing compliance is not achieved in any of the Schengen countries, contradicting the claim that Schengen routing already was a factual reality today, as it has been stated by the Association of the German Internet Industry [4]. Therefore, intelligence agencies still can perform potential wiretapping activities outside the Schengen jurisdiction on traffic originating within and destined to the Schengen Area.

This work and chkroute especially with the data set collected only analyze traffic in the forward direction. The reverse path may not necessarily be the same [11]. Hence, future work will address the reverse path, too. Furthermore, as only routes originating in Schengen countries targeted at a single node in Switzerland have been analyzed, results may differ, if a target node in another country was chosen. In particular, routes originating in a Schengen country A may be more or less likely than those originating in another Schengen country B to traverse a non-Schengen country depending on the location of the target node. Finally, an additional extension to this work is to analyze traffic for individual countries in more detail as well as to provide details with respect to countries that cause routes to be non-compliant with Schengen routing. It is also essential to identify those Schengen countries that are exit and entry points for traffic out of the Schengen Area and to examine the reason why this is the case.

Acknowledgments. This work was partially supported by the SmartenIT and the FLAMINGO projects, funded by the EU FP7 Program under Contract No. FP7-2012-ICT-317846 and No. FP7-2012-ICT-318488, respectively.

References

1. Augustin, B., Cuvellier, X., Orgogozo, B., Viger, F., Friedman, T., Latapy, M., Magnien, C., Teixeira, R.: Avoiding Traceroute Anomalies with Paris Traceroute. In: 6th ACM SIGCOMM Conference on Internet Measurement (IMC 2006), Rio de Janeiro, Brazil, pp. 153–158 (2006)
2. Blau, J.: NSA Surveillance Sparks Talk of National Internets. IEEE Spectrum 51, 14–16 (2014)
3. Bourgeau, T.: Monitoring Network Topology Dynamism of Large-scale Traceroute-based Measurements. In: 7th IEEE International Conference on Network and Service Management, Paris, France, pp. 489–493 (October 2011)
4. Computerwoche: Internet-Verband ECO Beklagt Scheindiskussion um "Schengen-Routing", http://www.computerwoche.de/a/internet-verband-eco-beklagt-scheindiskussion-um-schengen-routing,2556658 (last accessed: Feburary 2015)
5. D. Dönni, G.S. Machado: Traceroute Measurements in Schengen Area, http://www.csg.uzh.ch/publications/data/traceroute-schengen/ (last accessed: Feburary 2015)
6. Dönni, D.: chkroute utility, https://cms.uzh.ch/lenya/csg/authoring/publications/software/chkroute.html (last accessed: March 2015)
7. Banerjee, S., Griffin, T.G., Pias, M.: The Interdomain Connectivity of PlanetLab Nodes. In: Barakat, C., Pratt, I. (eds.) PAM 2004. LNCS, vol. 3015, pp. 73–82. Springer, Heidelberg (2004)
8. EMANICSLab, http://www.emanicslab.org (last accessed: December 2014)
9. European Commission: The Schengen Area, http://biblio.ucv.ro/bib_web/bib_pdf/EU_books/0056.pdf (last accessed: Feburary 2015)
10. Maxmind: GeoLite Legacy Downloadable Databases, http://dev.maxmind.com/geoip/legacy/geolite (last accessed: December 2014)
11. He, Y., Faloutsos, M., Krishnamurthy, S., Huffaker, B.: On Routing Asymmetry in the Internet. In: Global Telecommunications Conference (GLOBECOM 2005), St. Louis, USA, vol. 2, p. 6 (2005)
12. Hyun, Y., Broido, A., Claffy, K.C.: Traceroute and BGP AS Path Incongruities, Cooperative Association for Internet Data Analysis (CAIDA), Technical Report (March 2003), http://www.caida.org/publications/papers/2003/ASP/asp-incon.pdf (last accessed: February 2015)
13. Landau, S.: Making Sense from Snowden: What's Significant in the NSA Surveillance Revelations. Journal of Security Privacy 11(4), 54–63 (2013)

14. OpenWRT, https://openwrt.org (last accessed: January 2015)
15. Planet-Lab, https://www.planet-lab.org (last accessed: December 2014)
16. Pohlmann, N., Sparenberg, M., Siromaschenko, I., Kilden, K.: Secure Communications and Digital Sovereignty in Europe. In: ISSE 2014 Securing Electronic Business Processes, Brussels, Belgium, pp. 155–169 (2014)
17. RIPE NCC: RIPE ATLAS, http://atlas.ripe.net (last accessed: December 2014)
18. Sundaresan, S., Burnett, S., Feamster, N., De Donato, W.: BISmark: A Testbed for Deploying Measurements and Applications in Broadband Access Networks. In: 2014 USENIX Conference, San Diego, USA, pp. 383–394 (August 2014)
19. Zhang, Y., Oliveira, R., Zhang, H., Zhang, L.: Quantifying the Pitfalls of Traceroute in AS Connectivity Inference. In: Krishnamurthy, A., Plattner, B. (eds.) PAM 2010. LNCS, vol. 6032, pp. 91–100. Springer, Heidelberg (2010)

How Asymmetric Is the Internet?
A Study to Support the Use of Traceroute

Wouter de Vries, José Jair Santanna, Anna Sperotto[(⊠)], and Aiko Pras

University of Twente,
Design and Analysis of Communication Systems (DACS),
Enschede, The Netherlands
w.b.devries-1@student.utwente.nl
{a.sperotto,j.j.santanna,a.pras}@utwente.nl

Abstract. A network path is a path that a packet takes to reach its target. However, determining the network path that a host uses to reach it's target from the viewpoint of the latter is less trivial than it appears. Tools such as Traceroute allow the user to determine the path towards a target (i.e. the forward path), but not the path from the target to the source (i.e. the reverse path) due to routing asymmetry. Routing asymmetry means that the network path between two hosts may be different in opposite directions. Although previous studies have shown that this asymmetry is widespread, a more detailed characterization is lacking. In this paper routing asymmetry is investigated in depth using large scale measurements with 4.000 probes distributed world wide. The main goal of this paper is to provide characteristics about Internet asymmetry based on recent large scale measurements. Our findings contribute to a conclusive overview of Internet asymmetry, which assist researchers and engineers in making valid assumptions about routing asymmetry.

Keywords: Internet · Asymmetry · Large Scale Measurements

1 Introduction

The fact that Internet routing shows some degree of asymmetry has long been known [4,5,9,10]. Routing asymmetry means that, given two hosts A and B, the path from A to B (the forward path) is different from the the path from B to A (the reverse path). Asymmetry can, for example, be problematic when trying to troubleshoot problems at host A that occur on the reverse path. The reason for this is that standard tools, such as Traceroute, are only able to determine the forward path from the viewpoint of host A.

There have been various studies that quantify Internet routing asymmetry. This study aims to reinforce those studies and provide a more in depth analysis to determine where exactly this asymmetry occurs. A better understanding of the characteristics of Internet asymmetry can, for example, help when attempting to troubleshoot problems that occur on the reverse path when only the forward path is known.

© IFIP International Federation for Information Processing 2015
S. Latré et al. (Eds.): AIMS 2015, LNCS 9122, pp. 113–125, 2015.
DOI: 10.1007/978-3-319-20034-7_12

In this paper we look into the asymmetry of network paths. We investigate to what extent the reverse path can still be determined using the forward path if the characteristics of Internet asymmetry are known. The goal of this study is to provide an in depth analysis of Internet routing asymmetry. To perform this analysis we measure network paths between 4.000 probes across the world. We analyze the resulting data for network path asymmetry from the Autonomous System (AS) level. We show that most routes are not completely symmetrical, although the routes do have properties that still make them useful for specific applications, such as troubleshooting and collaboration with upstream providers. The contribution of this paper is providing information that researchers and engineers can use for the practical applicability of forward/reverse paths.

This paper is organized as follows. In Section 2 we discuss the related work followed by Section 3, where we explain our hypothesis. In Section 4 we describe our data acquisition. Then, in Section 5, the analysis will be described. Finally, we will present our conclusions in Section 6.

2   Related Work

Researchers have been studying Internet routing asymmetry for some time [4, 5, 7, 10]. In this section we will discuss a few studies that have investigated the level of routing asymmetry on the Internet and indicate what shortcomings they have that we aimed to solve.

First, the research in [5] on route asymmetry covers the AS level. They conclude that route asymmetry, on the AS level, is only present in approximately 14% of the routes. However, this research is based on results gathered using the Active Measurement Project (AMP) which runs mainly on academic networks and uses only 135 probes. In their follow up study [4], they use 350 probes selected from 1200 public traceroute servers. They note that the routing asymmetry percentage is much higher on commercial networks, namely 65%, which negatively impacts the usability of Traceroute to measure reverse network paths.

In addition, while they have conducted extensive research on route asymmetry on the AS level they have not looked at the relative position of asymmetry (e.g. close to the target of the traceroute, in the middle or close to the source of the traceroute). If we are interested in the remaining usability of reverse paths this is an interesting measurement, for example for applications that do not require the entire path to be symmetric. They proposed an interesting framework for quantifying the change in paths in which they use the the Levenshtein Edit Distance (ED) algorithm as a way to determine the distance between two paths.

Secondly, research in [10] concluded that the asymmetry on the AS level is substantially higher than in [4, 5]. According to them, asymmetry on the AS level is as high as 90%. The cause of this difference could, for example, be that this study was conducted 5 years later or that their dataset is obtained using only a total of 220 probes biased distributed.

Finally, the research in [7] proposes a way of determining the actual path that a packet has taken to reach a point in a network, with routing asymmetry in mind, from the viewpoint of the receiver. They do this mainly for troubleshooting purposes (e.g. which network is dropping packets). Their method involves a system of widely deployed probes, IP spoofing and the use of an option in the IP header that is often not implemented. While the theory behind this method is sound, it can be difficult to deploy in practice for a few reasons. First, potential users need to have widely deployed probes in place. Secondly, their method uses the Record Route option in the IP header. However, this option is often ignored [6] and packets that use this option are usually dropped. Finally, the use of IP spoofing, the act of forging the source address, can be problematic due to issues with company policies, ethics and the fact that there are techniques to block IP spoofing such as proposed in Request for Comment (RFC) 2827 [2], which is currently known as Best Current Practice (BCP) 38.

3   Hypothesis

The goal of this section is to describe some terminology and concepts. Then, we will introduce the hypothesis.

In this paper we consider a *network path* an ordered list of networks that connect two end-systems on the Internet. Although there are studies that differentiate networks by IP address or even as IP address range [4], we chose to represent networks as Autonomous System (Autonomous System (AS)). By using ASes it is trivial to cluster IP addresses that belong to the same administrative network.

As shown in Fig. 1 there are two distinct paths between a pair of end-systems A and B: The forward path and the reverse path. When both paths are completely equal then the path is symmetric, otherwise it is asymmetric. Note that to reliably determine a complete network path from the viewpoint of the receiver, the Internet would have to be completely symmetric.

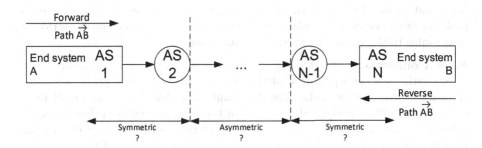

Fig. 1. Network path

Our goal is to show that network paths are symmetric near the end-systems, meaning that for that section of the network path standard tools can be used to determine the reverse path. We defined the following hypothesis: *The reverse network path can be reliably discovered via standard tools, such as Traceroute, near the end-systems..*

4   Data Acquisition

In this section we will describe the methodology that we used. We will first explain which measurement network we use and what it consists of. Then, we will explain how the measurements are configured. Lastly, we will present some preliminary considerations concerning the measurements.

The main requirement for investigating our hypothesis was having a large amount of Internet connected computer systems which we could control. In order to meet this requirement we use RIPE Atlas. This project manages probes around the world for the specific purpose of network measurements. A probe is a dedicated network measurement device that can be placed in a network to allow measurements to be performed remotely. The Atlas project consists of approximately 7.000 distributed probes[1] worldwide. Although we are aware of several other measurement infrastructures, such as PlanetLAB[2], EmanicsLAB[3] and the NLNOG Ring[4], these do not provide the scale and distribution that was required for measurements that are representative of the Internet.

RIPE Atlas has imposed a credit system that limits measurements in three ways. The credits that are consumed per day, the number of measurements that can be run concurrently and the total number of credits that can be consumed. These limits have a consequence on the number of probes that can be used and in which combination. Credits can, for example, be earned by hosting a RIPE Atlas probe. It is due this credit limit that not all probes that are available can be used. This further depends on the measurement layout, which probe measures what and to what other probe.

4.1   Measurement Configuration

We considered three layouts in which the probes can conduct the measurements. Note that to be able to determine route asymmetry between two probes, each probe has to traceroute the other. In the considered layouts each probe performs traceroutes to the probes to which it is connected.

Fully Connected Layout (Fig. 2a) - This layout has the advantage of utilizing the complete potential of the involved probes, every probe measures the path to every other probe. The disadvantage is that due to the credit limit only a very limited amount of probes from the total can be used. For example: considering the 1 million credit limit only 112 probes can be used due to the high amount of paths in this type of layout. A small amount of probes means that specific network issues that occur at individual probes have a large impact.

Star Layout (Fig. 2b) - In comparison to the fully connected topology this has the advantage of allowing many more probes to be used. However, in this

---

[1] RIPE Atlas System Statistics:https://atlas.ripe.net/

[2] https://www.planet-lab.org/

[3] http://www.emanicslab.org/

[4] https://ring.nlnog.net/

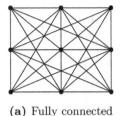
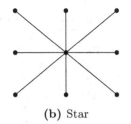
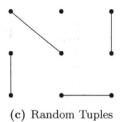

(a) Fully connected   **(b)** Star   **(c)** Random Tuples

Fig. 2. Probe layout

case the center probe will have a large impact on each measurement. Network issues at the center probe can cause the entire experiment to fail.

Random Tuple Layout (Fig. 2c) - In this layout random tuples of probes are selected. This has the advantage of minimizing the impact of a single misbehaving probe. Furthermore, it allows for a much larger selection of probes, considering the Atlas limits. Because of these advantages this is the layout that we used.

Using the random tuple layout we selected 4.000 probes, meaning 2.000 tuples, in a way that favoured longer geographic distances. The attempt to have longer geographic distances is to prevent a large concentration of probes in Europe, as most probes are located there. The algorithm used to select the probes works by randomly picking probes and comparing the distance between them to some threshold (in our case: 10.000 km), if the threshold is exceeded then the probe tuple is added to the final result set. If, after a number of attempts (in our case: 2.000), no probe tuples can be found that exceed the threshold then the threshold will be lowered.

The distribution over continents in terms of numbers is shown in Table 1. There is a large skew towards Europe which is caused by the relatively large number of probes located there. The average distance between two probes in a tuple is 6.945 kilometres (as the crow flies).

For every selected pair consisting of probe A and probe B two measurements were scheduled. One measurement, consisting of a traceroute, was configured from probe A to probe B (the forward path) and another from probe B to probe A (the reverse path).

Network variances over time were smoothed out by scheduling the measurements to run every three hours, for ten days. This was limited by the total amount of credits we were allowed to consume. The measurements were performed from 14:00 on the 28th of July 2014 to 14:00 on the 7th of August 2014, Coordinated Universal Time (UTC).

4.2   Preliminary Considerations

RIPE Atlas probes conduct their traces on the IP level where each hop consists of a single IP address. Because we want to look at the network paths from the

Table 1. Distribution over continents

Continent	Selected	Available	Fraction	Fraction of selected
Europe	2681	5200	51.56%	67.03%
North America	724	1003	72.18%	18.10%
Asia	267	420	63.57%	6.68%
Africa	157	223	70.40%	3.93%
Oceania	109	145	75.17%	2.73%
South America	59	87	67.82%	1.48%
Antarctica	1	1	100.00%	0.03%
Unknown	*2*	*4*	*50.00%*	*0.05%*
Total	*4000*	*7083*		*100%*

AS level it was necessary to convert the measured paths. In order to convert IP addresses to their corresponding AS numbers we used the BGP routing table dumps obtained from the Remote Route Collector (RRC)s managed by the Routing Information Service (RIS), which in turn is operated by RIPE. These routing tables contain a large amount of routes that are announced on the Internet by different ASes. Using these routes we are able to determine the AS number for a given IP range. The tool we used for this and its source is available online[5]. Alternatives to this method are, for example, provided by CAIDA[6] or MaxMind[7].

Each IP address in the paths on the router level was converted to their corresponding AS number. It is apparently common for multiple hops to occur within the same network. This is shown by the reduction in the number of hops in network paths on the router level in comparison to network paths on the AS level, which is, on average, 64.46%.

Our choice of probes was optimized to prevent a large cluster of probes in Europe by increasing the geographic distance between pairs, this may have introduced a bias in network path length. In order to show that this is not the case we plot the geographic distance, which is shortest distance between two points on a sphere (great circle distance), against the number of hops in the forward network path on the AS level. The result of this is shown in Fig. 3. As we expected there appears to be no clear relation between the geographic distance and the number of hops.

In Fig. 4 the distribution of the length of the measured paths is shown. Most paths contain five different AS-numbers. This means that in those cases three autonomous systems aside from the one the receiver and the sender are in (e.g. their ISPs) are involved in routing the packets.

The measurements that were performed by the probes were not completely perfect or complete. This may, for example, have been caused by probes that delayed their measurements for too long or did not perform them at all. Because of this we have applied some filters to the dataset. Prior to the filtering we

---

[5] IPASNExporter: https://bitbucket.org/woutifier/ipasnexporter

[6] http://www.caida.org/

[7] https://www.maxmind.com/

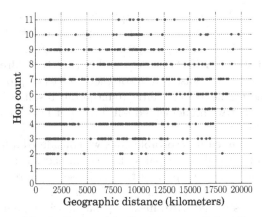

Fig. 3. Geographic distance vs path length

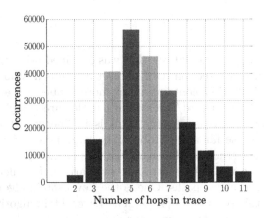

Fig. 4. Distribution of path length

had 153,638 potential forward/reverse path pairs, of a theoretical 160,000. The absence of some paths can be attributed to some probes that did not respond or did not complete any measurements.

Since forward and reverse path measurements are initiated from two different probes there can be a delay between the two measurements being executed. To prevent this difference from influencing the results we only match paths if they were measured no more than 600 seconds apart. If they are outside that time limit the forward/reverse pair is discarded. This prevents path instability from being interpreted as path asymmetry. This filter reduced our potential forward/reverse path pairs by 16,103.

The second filter we implemented is based on the principle that the first hop of the forward path should be the last hop of the reverse path, because these are the origin and destination networks. The same principle applies in the opposite direction. Measurements where this is not the case can be caused by incomplete traces. We filtered all forward/reverse path pairs where this was the case. This removed 14,620 results from the set.

To prevent probes that measured completely empty paths to influence the results we filtered all pairs that contained a completely empty path. Completely empty paths do not exist in actual networks, as a network path always contains at least a single hop, even if the source and target IP addresses are in the same network. This can be caused by incomplete traces or probes that are not executing their measurements. This filter reduced our result set by 3,365.

The three filters that we implemented left a total of 119,550 or 74.72% of the theoretical 160,000 pairs.

For paths that contained unresolvable hops we considered a few options. The first option is to discard all path pairs that contained such a hop. However, this would impact a significant part of the result set as unresolvable hops are common. Another option, which was also implemented in [3] is to simply consider an unresolvable hop as a wild card, meaning that it will match any hop in the opposite path that is in the same position.

5   Analysis

In this section we analyze the dataset that was obtained using the methodology described in the previous section. Our dataset contains a total of 2275 unique AS numbers, of which 1717 contain one or more probes. Of all results in our dataset, 15053 (12.6%) forward/reverse path tuples are completely symmetric and 104497 (87.4%) show asymmetry. This is in line with the results found in [10], however, we use far more probes. The large percentage of asymmetric paths further justifies studying the characteristics of Internet asymmetry.

Before we start the analysis we introduce two variants for calculating the Edit Distance (ED) between two paths. One is the Levenshtein algorithm [8] which was first used for this purpose in [4] [5]. The Levenshtein algorithm counts the number of required insert, delete or change operations to make two paths equal to each other. The Levenshtein algorithm was originally intended to be used to measure the differences between strings, however, it can be used without modification for measuring the change in network paths. In addition to the Levenshtein algorithm we also use a variation called Damerau-Levenshtein [1]. Damerau-Levenshtein extends the original algorithm by also counting transpose operations as a single change. It is much less sensitive to swapped hops. The extended algorithm is interesting in contexts where the presence of ASes on a path are of more importance than their specific location.

5.1   Stability Over Time

We begin our investigation by determining the change of paths over time. This is of interest because it is not always possible to measure the reverse path at the exact time that the forward path was established. We calculate the average ED over all paths over time. The ED is determined as follows: The first path to a destination is taken as a ground truth to which each consecutive path is compared. We then calculate the ED based on the Levenshtein algorithm. We

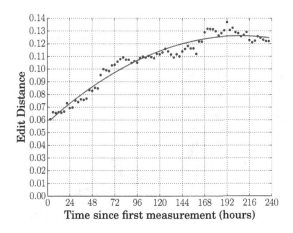

Fig. 5. ED over time using Levenshtein algorithm

had to modify the algorithm slightly because not all paths are of the same length, which would cause longer paths to have a much higher impact on the results than shorter paths. Therefore, we normalize the ED by dividing it by the path length as shown in formula 1.

$$\frac{ED(forward, reverse)}{MAX(len(forward), len(reverse))} \tag{1}$$

The normalized ED is between 0.0 (i.e. completely symmetric) and 1.0 (i.e. completely asymmetric). Fig. 5 shows the results of this analysis. Note that the graphs indicate that network paths are not subject to great change over time. The instability appears to stop increasing after 8 days, therefore measurements should be done over a longer period of time to show if this behavior persists. Furthermore, we compared the results using the Levenshtein algorithm to the Damerau-Levenshtein algorithm and this showed results which are almost completely identical. This indicates that the relative position of a network in a path is stable.

5.2   Absolute Difference

We look at the absolute difference between the forward and reverse path pairs to get an understanding of how big the impact of routing asymmetry is. We define the absolute difference as the ED between the forward and reverse path. The ED between all path pairs is shown in Fig. 6. Note that the difference between the results of the two algorithms indicates that it is a common occurrence for two hops to be swapped in either the forward or reverse path. Furthermore, most forward/reverse path pairs show a distance of either 1 or 2 from their counterpart.

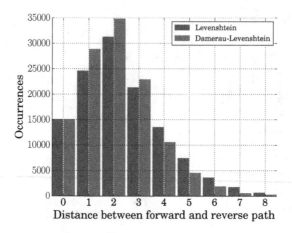

Fig. 6. Distance between forward and reverse path

5.3 Relative difference by position

In this section we show the similarity of hops based on their relative position in the path. This shows if a certain hop is usable for mitigation. If a forward and reverse trace have different lengths then they are not included in this figure, which results in 28139 result pairs being used in Fig. 7. This shows how the symmetry decreases as we move closer to the middle of the path, as expected. It also shows that for the longest path (7 hops) the middle hop is equal in both the forward and reverse path in approximately 60% of the cases.

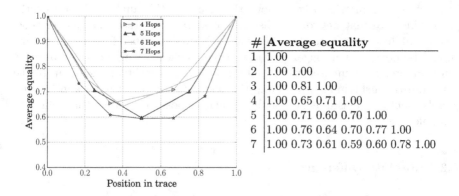

Fig. 7. Average equality by position in trace

Given this measure of asymmetry we try to find out if the majority of asymmetry is caused by a small number of networks (i.e. ASes). We look at which ASes are involved when asymmetry occurs. From the approximately 500 ASes that are involved we see that the top 10 is responsible for 48% of the total asymmetry. We manually categorized these ten ASes in three types: T1 for Tier 1

Table 2. Top 10 ASes involved in asymmetry

Position	ASN	Name	Type
1	3356	Level 3 Communications, Inc.	T1
2	174	Cogent Communications	T1
3	1299	TeliaSonera International Carrier	T1
4	3257	Tinet SpA	T1
5	3216	OJSC Vimpelcom	T2
6	34984	TELLCOM ILETISIM HIZMETLERI A.S.	T2
7	1200	Amsterdam Internet Exchange B.V.	IXP
8	2914	NTT America, Inc.	T1
9	6453	TATA Communications, Inc.	T1
10	6695	DE-CIX Management GmbH	IXP

providers, T2 for Large ISPs and IXP for Internet Exchange Points. The results are shown in Table 2. It is obvious that the largest Internet Service Provides (i.e. Tier 1 providers), cause the largest part of the asymmetry. It is likely that this is because those providers are also the ones which have the most peering connections.

5.4   Consecutive Equal Hops

We count the number Consecutive Equal Hops (CEH) from each side of the forward/reverse path that are equal, not counting the source and target networks. This approach can be used even if the lengths of the forward/reverse path are unequal. The average number of CEH, divided by two to get an average for each side, is plotted against the total number of hops in the forward path in Fig. 8a.

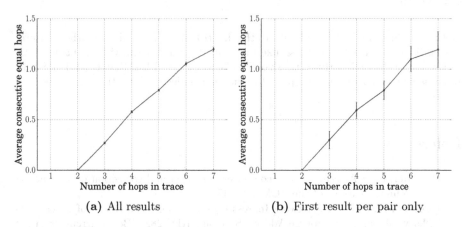

(a) All results   (b) First result per pair only

Fig. 8. Average number of CEH between forward and reverse paths

Included in Fig. 8a is the 95% confidence interval. This figure shows that for path lengths 6 and 7 there is on average at least one additional equal network aside from the source and target networks. For the most common path length, five, there is one network that is the same in both the forward and reverse path in approximately 75% of the cases.

In Fig. 8b only the first complete result for each pair is considered. These graphs show that it is not necessary to do repeated measurements over a longer period of time to determine route asymmetry. Note that this suggests that route asymmetry does not vary significantly over time.

6   Conclusion

In this paper we have analyzed and characterized several aspects of Internet routing asymmetry. Our analysis has been conducted on a large scale using RIPE Atlas. The results from our study contribute to assist researchers and engineers in making valid assumptions while using forward/reverse paths data. In addition, we contribute to give a conclusive overview on the partial asymmetry of Internet routing.

The usability of Traceroute for measuring reverse paths is, depending on the application, questionable. We have confirmed the presence of asymmetry in the majority of Internet routes, and determined where this asymmetry occurs. Our hypothesis, that reverse network paths can be reliably discovered via standard tools near the end-systems has been confirmed. We have found, in the worst case, a hop, representing an AS, is the same in the forward and the reverse path in 59% of the cases, but often more.

As future work we plan to extend the analysis on the IP-level. Furthermore, we plan to apply machine learning to estimate network path accuracy given certain indicators, such as the type of networks that are involved and the length of the path.

Acknowledgments. We would like to thank RIPE Atlas for facilitating the measurements. In addition, we would also like to thank Roland van Rijswijk for his insights. This work was funded by the Network of Excellence project FLAMINGO (ICT-318488), which is supported by the European Commission under its Seventh Framework Programme.

References

1. Damerau, F.J.: A technique for computer detection and correction of spelling errors. Communications of the ACM 7(3), 171–176 (1964)
2. Ferguson, P., Senie, D.: Network Ingress Filtering: Defeating Denial of Service Attacks which employ IP Source Address Spoofing. RFC 2827 (Best Current Practice) (2000), http://www.ietf.org/rfc/rfc2827.txt
3. He, Y.H.Y., Chen, W.C.W., Xiao, B.X.B., Peng, W.P.W.: An Efficient and Practical Defense Method Against DDoS Attack at the Source-End. In: 11th International Conference on Parallel and Distributed Systems (ICPADS 2005) (February 2005)

4. He, Y., Faloutsos, M., Krishnamurthy, S., Huffaker, B.: On routing asymmetry in the Internet. In: Global Telecommunications Conference, GLOBECOM 2005, vol. 2, p. 6. IEEE (November 2005)
5. He, Y., Faloutsos, M., Krishnamurthy, S.V.: Quantifying routing asymmetry in the Internet at the AS level. In: GLOBECOM, pp. 1474–1479. IEEE (2004), http://dblp.uni-trier.de/db/conf/globecom/globecom2004.html#HeFK04
6. Iputils: ping(8) (2014), http://man7.org/linux/man-pages/man8/ping.8.html
7. Katz-Bassett, E., Madhyastha, H., Adhikari, V.: Reverse traceroute. In: Network Systems Design and Implementation (2010), https://www.usenix.org/legacy/event/nsdi10/tech/full_papers/katz-bassett.pdf
8. Levenshtein, V.I.: Binary codes capable of correcting deletions, insertions, and reversals. Soviet Physics Doklady 10, 707–710 (1966)
9. Paxson, V.: End-to-end Routing Behavior in the Internet. In: Conference Proceedings on Applications, Technologies, Architectures, and Protocols for Computer Communications, SIGCOMM 1996, pp. 25–38. ACM, New York (1996), http://doi.acm.org/10.1145/248156.248160
10. Schwartz, Y., Shavitt, Y., Weinsberg, U.: On the Diversity, Stability and Symmetry of End-to-End Internet Routes. In: INFOCOM IEEE Conference on Computer Communications Workshops 2010, pp. 1–6 (2010)

Ph.D. Student Workshop — Security Management

Mitigating DDoS Attacks Using OpenFlow-Based Software Defined Networking

Mattijs Jonker[(✉)] and Anna Sperotto

Design and Analysis of Communication Systems (DACS),
Centre for Telematics and Information Technology (CTIT),
University of Twente, Enschede, The Netherlands
{m.jonker,a.sperotto}@utwente.nl

Abstract. Over the last years, Distributed Denial-of-Service (DDoS) attacks have become an increasing threat on the Internet, with recent attacks reaching traffic volumes of up to *500 Gbps*. To make matters worse, web-based facilities that offer "DDoS-as-a-service" (i.e., *Booters*) allow for the layman to launch attacks in the order of tens of *Gbps* in exchange for only a few euros. A recent development in networking is the principle of Software Defined Networking (SDN), and related technologies such as OpenFlow. In SDN, the control plane and data plane of the network are decoupled. This has several advantages, such as centralized control over forwarding decisions, dynamic updating of forwarding rules, and easier and more flexible network configuration. Given these advantages, we expect SDN to be well-suited for DDoS attack mitigation. Typical mitigation solutions, however, are not built using SDN. In this paper we propose to design and to develop an OpenFlow-based mitigation architecture for DDoS attacks. The research involves looking at the applicability of OpenFlow, as well as studying existing solutions built on other technologies. The research is as yet in its beginning phase and will contribute towards a Ph.D. thesis after four years.

1 Introduction

While Distributed Denial-of-Service (DDoS) attacks have been long noted in the literature, it was not until a large group of attacks referred to as *"operation payback"* in 2010 by WikiLeaks supporters that the general public better understood the power of such attacks. As part of this group of attacks, the websites of *MasterCard* and *Visa* were brought down entirely, and *PayPal*'s website was notably disrupted [1,2]. Ever since, we have seen a rapid increase in DDoS attacks in occurrence and magnitude. The *"Spamhaus attack"* is a notorious example [3]. While its *300 Gbps* traffic peak created the largest-ever-seen DDoS attack at the time, it has since been surpassed by attacks up to sheer volumes of *500 Gbps* [4,5]. These types of attacks use core parts of the Internet infrastructure to amplify traffic (e.g., the *Domain Name System (DNS)*) and can be launched without an underlying botnet. As they operate at the network and transport layers [6], they are nearly impossible to mitigate with strictly on-premise solutions. To make matters worse, the ability to launch such attacks is

© IFIP International Federation for Information Processing 2015
S. Latré et al. (Eds.): AIMS 2015, LNCS 9122, pp. 129–133, 2015.
DOI: 10.1007/978-3-319-20034-7_13

nowadays no longer limited to people with advanced technical skills. Contrarily, "DDoS-as-a-Service" providers, i.e., *Booters* [7], allow anyone to perform attacks in the order of tens of Gbps in exchange for only a few euros. As a result of the increased threat of DDoS attacks, a market for mitigation solutions was created, which gave rise to DDoS Protection Service (DPS) providers such as *Akamai Prolexic* [8], *CloudFlare* [9] and *Verisign* [10].

A recent development in networking technology that has attracted a lot of attention from the research community is the Software Defined Networking (SDN) principle [11,12]. In SDN, the control plane and data plane of the network are decoupled. This decoupling has many advantages, such as centralized control over forwarding decisions, dynamic updating of forwarding rules, and easier and more flexible network configuration. OpenFlow [13] is the most commonly deployed SDN technology. Considering the characteristics of SDN, we expect it to be well-suited for DDoS attack mitigation [14].

Despite SDN's potential for DDoS attack mitigation [15], we observe that existing solutions rely on other techniques. For example, solutions offered by 'cloud-based' DPS providers rely on DNS anycast and Border Gateway Protocol (BGP) announcements. Moreover, there are challenges when it comes to SDN itself, such as the performance of programmable devices, and its susceptibility to attacks [16,17]. The aim of this research, therefore, is to investigate the applicability of OpenFlow-enabled SDN for DDoS attack mitigation, and to propose and develop an architecture to this end.

The remainder of this paper is organized as follows. In Section 2 the research questions and approach for this work are detailed. Some of the preliminary steps taken are presented in Section 3, and in Section 4 we conclude this paper.

2   Goal, Research Questions and Approach

The goal of this research is to evaluate OpenFlow for use in DDoS attack mitigation, and to design and to develop a mitigation architecture. By using the advantages of OpenFlow, such an architecture is expected to allow for attacks to be mitigated in an early stage, i.e., closer to the Internet backbone and further away from the target, in a flexible and scalable manner. In addition, an OpenFlow-based architecture may allow, to some extent, the protected entity to control routing, which could have benefits. In support of achieving this goal we have defined the following main research question.

> RQ_M : Can we use OpenFlow in a DDoS attack mitigation architecture, and how will such an architecture operate?

Our approach to answering RQ_M is primarily measurement-based, in which measurements are first focussed on assessing the applicability of OpenFlow-enabled devices for DDoS mitigation, and later shift towards the architecture operation. In the subsections to follow we will divide the main research question in sub-questions, and discuss, for every sub-question, the envisioned approach.

2.1   The Applicability of OpenFlow-Based SDN

In the context of researching the applicability of OpenFlow-based SDN for a mitigation architecture, the following sub-questions are defined.

> $RQ_{M.1}$: **What do DDoS attack mitigation solutions based on technologies other than SDN look like, and how do they operate?** The purpose of this research question is to thoroughly study other solutions, and investigate where OpenFlow-based SDN can excell, and where it may fall short in comparison. Typical solutions based on BGP and DNS anycast, for example, re-route all traffic at the network layer (L3) through 'scrubbing centers', i.e., data centers where traffic is cleansed. This way of operating needs to be studied for comparative purposes.
>
> $RQ_{M.2}$: **How applicable is OpenFlow to the end of DDoS attack mitigation, in terms of flexibility, performance, and scalability?** The specification of OpenFlow may be different from the performance and scalability actually offered by OpenFlow implementations. This question serves to quantify the flexibility, performance, and scalability of OpenFlow.

To approach $RQ_{M.1}$, we will study mitigation solutions offered by DPS providers; solutions deployed at backbone providers, ISPs, and National Research and Education Networks (NREN); and other type of solutions, such as traditional firewalls or vendor-specific solutions. Part of this study will include large-scale measurements using DNS, which will reveal statistics about which domains use (or migrate to) cloud-based DPS providers. Furthermore, using DNS we can study how parts of DPS architectures based on DNS anycast (e.g., *CloudFlare*) operate and behave. We will also perform comparative benchmarks between transport layer (L4) filtering with OpenFlow and traditional firewalls or vendor-specific implementations, such those based on [18]. We will also perform measurements to study if re-routing everything at L3 is efficient. Our approach for $RQ_{M.2}$ will include benchmarks of specific OpenFlow-enabled device implementations, for example to see how well forwarding devices behave when rules are frequently dynamically modified. This type of benchmarks will be done in lab settings, as well as in production networks.

2.2   Architecture Requirements

In the context of architecture requirements, the following sub-question is defined.

> $RQ_{M.3}$: **What are the requirements of an OpenFlow-based mitigation architecture for DDoS attacks?** This research question serves to get a thorough technical understanding of how an architecture needs to operate, what its performance requirements are, and how it can be scalable and be flexible. Its design should also account for the notion that multiple organisations are likely to be involved, which will give rise to legal and ethical questions, such as about net neutrality.

The approach we will take to answer $RQ_{M.3}$ involves interviewing operators of software defined networks [12] to reveal how current SDN topologies are deployed, what the challenges are, if and how control over routing is currently realized, and under which conditions dynamic routing allows for DDoS attack mitigation. Non-technical issues (e.g., ethical and legal) can also be identified this way. The approach also involves measurements of preliminary architecture setups in a lab setting to measure how different parts interact. This will allow us to benchmark architecture designs, review requirements, and steer architecture design choices.

The overall approach, as identified in the preceding sections, will be iterative. This is due to several reasons. First, the consequences of design choices may affect architecture scalability and performance. Second, results from one research question may lead to revisiting others.

3   Preliminary Steps

This section briefly describes some preliminary steps taken to achieve the goal of the proposed research. We recently deployed a large-scale measurement framework based on DNS. It uses the full *.com*, *.net* and *.org* zones to perform DNS queries for about *142* million domain names daily. Given that several record types are of interest, billions of queries are performed per day. The measurement framework is used for different research efforts, but in the context of this work it is used as follows. By mapping address responses of domains, i.e. A and AAAA to Autonomous System (AS) numbers, the use of DPS providers (e.g., *CloudFlare*) can be identified. Name Server (NS) responses can be used to the same end. This type of analysis allows us to evaluate statistics on the use of, and migration over time to, DPS providers.

4   Final Considerations

During the first four months of this Ph.D research, the preliminary steps presented in Section 3 were taken. The main goal of this work (as described in Section 2) should be achieved within a period of four years, as part of a Ph.D thesis. During this time, this research is expected to benefit from the network of contacts the University of Twente (UT) has, such as those in the context of EU FP7 FLAMINGO NoE.

Acknowledgments. This research is funded by FLAMINGO, a Network of Excellence project (318488) supported by the European Commission under its Seventh Framework Programme and by the NWO Project D3.

References

1. Addley, E., Halliday, J.: WikiLeaks supporters disrupt Visa and MasterCard sites in 'Operation Payback's,
http://www.theguardian.com/world/2010/dec/08/wikileaks-visa-mastercard
-operation-payback/ (accessed on January 13, 2015)

2. Greenberg, A.: WikiLeaks Supporters Aim Cyberattacks At PayPal, http://www.forbes.com/sites/andygreenberg/2010/12/06/wikileaks-supporters -aim-cyberattacks-at-paypal/ (accessed on January 13, 2015)
3. Markoff, J., Pelroth, N.: Firm Is Accused of Sending Spam, and Fight Jams Internet, http://www.nytimes.com/2013/03/27/technology/internet/online-dispute-becomes-internet-snarling-attack.html?_r=0 (accessed on January 13, 2015)
4. Musil, S.: Record-breaking DDoS attack in Europe hits 400Gbps, http://www.cnet.com/news/record-breaking-ddos-attack-in-europe-hits-400gbps/ (accessed on January 13, 2015)
5. Olson, P.: The Largest Cyber Attack In History Has Been Hitting Hong Kong Sites, http://www.forbes.com/sites/parmyolson/2014/11/20/the-largest-cyber-attack-in-history-has-been-hitting-hong-kong-sites/ (accessed on January 13, 2015)
6. Zimmermann, H.: OSI reference model–The ISO model of architecture for open systems interconnection. IEEE Transactions on Communications 28(4), 425–432 (1980)
7. Karami, M., McCoy, D.: Understanding the Emerging Threat of DDoS-as-a-Service. In: Proceedings of the 6th USENIX Workshop on Large-Scale Exploits and Emergent Threats, LEET 2013 (2013)
8. Prolexic, A.: Prolexic: DDoS Protection and Mitigation, http://www.prolexic.com/ (accessed on January 13, 2015)
9. CloudFlare: CloudFlare: The web performance & security company, http://www.cloudflare.com/ (accessed on January 13, 2015)
10. Verisign: Verisign: Internet Security and Web Domain Names, http://www.verisigninc.com/ (accessed on January 13, 2015)
11. Shenker, S., Casado, M., Koponen, T., McKeown, N.: The future of networking, and the past of protocols, Presented at the Open Networking Summit (2011)
12. Bezerra, J.A.: Migrating AmLight from legacy to SDN: Challenges, Results and Next Step, Presented at NANOG 63 (2015)
13. McKeown, N., Anderson, T., Balakrishnan, H., Parulkar, G., Peterson, L., Rexford, J., Shenker, S., Turner, J.: OpenFlow: enabling innovation in campus network. ACM SIGCOMM Computer Communication Review 38(2), 69–74 (2008)
14. François, J., Dolberg, L., Festor, O., Engel, T.: Network Security through Software Defined Networking: a Survey. In: Proceedings of the 7th ACM Conference on Principles, Systems and Applications of IP Telecommunications, IPTComm 2014 (2014)
15. Vizváry, M., Vykopal, J.: Future of DDoS Attacks Mitigation in Software Defined Networks. In: Sperotto, A., Doyen, G., Latré, S., Charalambides, M., Stiller, B. (eds.) AIMS 2014. LNCS, vol. 8508, pp. 123–127. Springer, Heidelberg (2014)
16. Sezer, S., Scott-Hayward, S., Kaur, P.C., Fraser, B., Lake, D., Finnegan, J., Viljoen, N., Miller, M., Roa, N.: Are We Ready for SDN? Implementation Challenges for Software-Defined Networks. ACM SIGCOMM Computer Communication Review 51(7), 36–43 (2013)
17. Kreutz, D., Ramos, F., Verissimo, P.: Towards secure and dependable software-defined networks. In: Proceedings of the 2nd ACM SIGCOMM Workshop on Hot Topics in Software Defined Networking (2013)
18. Juniper: Junos OS: Network operating system for routing, switching, and security, http://www.juniper.net/us/en/products-services/nos/junos/ (accessed on January 22, 2015)

Towards an Adaptive and Effective IDS Using OpenFlow

Sebastian Seeber[✉] and Gabi Dreo Rodosek

Department of Computer Science, Universität der Bundeswehr München,
85577 Neubiberg, Germany
{sebastian.seeber,gabi.dreo}@unibw.de

Abstract. Processing huge amounts of traffic from core network components with respect to security remains a challenging task, since the amounts of data increase continuously. Therefore, new approaches need to be investigated to detect and handle attacks already in high-speed environments. In this PhD research, we will develop a new approach for detecting network attacks by processing data from core network components taking advantage of properties of OpenFlow in an SDN environment. Using this, we can collect metadata about forwarded traffic in an immediate and effective way. In addition, our solution will enable dynamic and adaptive redirection of traffic to various IDSs including cloud-based IDS solutions.

1 Introduction and Motivation

Security at network level states an important research area since consumers and companies push their data continuously into cloud environments [5]. A reason for this evolution is the growing popularity of cloud services as well as simplicity and fast dynamic expandability of resources on demand. In addition, distributed denial-of-service (DDoS) attacks increased dramatically during the last years [2]. A recent report from Akamai [1] shows 90 % growth of DDoS attacks in the last 12 month. The advent of software defined networking (SDN) promises a large variety of possibilities to improve network monitoring and traffic steering. Nevertheless, widespread deployments using SDN principles are still rare and mostly static (proactive) configured.

Network security solutions are primarily based on inspecting traffic. The most well-known approaches are on the one hand analyzing whole packets using deep packet inspection (DPI) and on the other hand using rather statistical data provided by NetFlow/IPFIX techniques [12]. The operational environment affects the chosen traffic inspection method. Environments carrying fewer amounts of data (average bandwidth from few Mb/s to 1 Gb/s) are suitable for DPI [8] whereas high-throughput (up to 100 Gb/s) environments like Internet Exchange Points (IXP) have only a chance inspecting traffic using NetFlow/IPFIX [17] and even sampled. A drawback of the latter approaches lays in their design, because statistics are calculated after a flow is terminated (by flow aging, TCP

© IFIP International Federation for Information Processing 2015
S. Latré et al. (Eds.): AIMS 2015, LNCS 9122, pp. 134–139, 2015.
DOI: 10.1007/978-3-319-20034-7_14

session termination or fixed interval). Therefore, these introduce a delay in a subsequent detection process.

In contrast, OpenFlow is able to raise an event or update a flow counter at arrival time of a packet depending on a match or mismatch with respect to an existing or non-existing flow. Deployments of commercial existing intrusion detection systems are mostly implemented in a static manner. If multiple Intrusion Detection Systems (IDSs) exist, traffic redirection is mainly based on subnets or IP addresses.

Our proposed effective IDS uses OpenFlow as a key-enabler and is adaptive since it involves multiple IDSs on-demand by taking into account immediate detection results. Keeping these thoughts in mind, the following research questions arise and need to be investigated:

RQ1 *How to use OpenFlow to gather statistics to detect attacks/anomalies?*
RQ2 *How to find an optimal trade-off between performance and detection rate?*
RQ3 *How to classify attack and reason suitable IDS and their sequence?*
RQ4 *How to compare cloud security solutions and how to validate them?*
RQ5 *How to verify the chosen path (Service Chain Verification)?*

The remainder of the paper is organized as follows. Section 2 discusses related work. We introduce our approach in Section 3. Concluding remarks and future work are described in Section 4.

2   Related Work

The use of SDN concepts towards network security is not new. Kreutz et al. [14] argue for building dependable and secure SDN applications. Therefore, they identified and described current threat vectors in SDN environments that could be exploited and propose a general design to overcome these threats. Besides this Scott et al. [16] investigated possible new security issues introduced through SDN and identified affected layers. François et al. [11] reviewed SDN security approaches according to their scope, practicability and advantages.

Research also has been done focusing on more specific attacks and their mitigation. Using self organizing maps the authors of [9] propose a method to detect DDoS attacks based on flow analysis. Feamster et al. [10] and Schehlmann et al. [15] investigated possibilities to detect botnet traffic by using distributed monitoring approaches. Combining traditional network features (sFlow) and OpenFlow, Giotis et al. [13] proposed a mechanism to detect anomalies and mitigate attacks by modifying flow tables.

3   Approach

The research in this PhD presents a new approach in providing security on the network level. To overcome existing static security function deployments, our approach provides security functions in a dynamic and free composable manner. Traditional approaches follow a static sequence of different security functions based on parameters like state of protective system, anticipated attack probability or expected risk-level. Instead, the mechanism concatenates security functions (e.g., various specialized IDSs) based on immediate detection results. OpenFlow is a well-established protocol in SDN deployments and therefore the most suitable enabler for our approach.

Overall Architecture. Our proposed overall architecture is depicted in Figure 1. Starting from left, the input traffic reaches a network core OpenFlow enabled switch (OF-Switch). It is important that this switch is as near as possible to an IXP to cope with large amounts of attack traffic. On top of this switch a light IDS (OF-IDS) is implemented using OpenFlow counters (*Meter-, Group-, Flow-Table* - OpenFlow 1.3) as input data. RQ1 and RQ2 are related to the development of an effective IDS based on monitoring data from an OpenFlow enabled switch.

Triggered by events of OF-IDS the connected SDN-Controller (SDN-C) processes the event provided by the IDS and information from the associated flow in order to decide about the subsequent detection step. RQ3 will answer this question by using traffic and attack characterization techniques to introduce adaptiveness. After a decision is taken by the SDN-C, OpenFlow rules are applied to the underlying OF-Switch meeting the decision requirements. The procedure between incoming traffic at the OF-Switch and SDN-C decision (including applying OpenFlow rules) will be called detection cycle (DC). The described behavior repeats at every point an IDS (IDS-A, IDS-B, IDS-C) is present. Various DCs are conceivable, depending on the number of available IDSs and detection results. In cases where not only on-site IDSs, like Suricata [7], SNORT [6] or Bro [3] are considered, the architecture is flexible in including cloud-based IDS solutions (Cloud-IDS), e.g., Cloudflare [4]. For example, the red-dotted line shows a case where only on-site IDSs are involved, whereas the green path involves a cloud-based IDS. Therefore, RQ4 investigates techniques to evaluate cloud security solutions (cloud-based IDS) and comparison criteria. It's important to mention, that only attack traffic is redirected to cloud-based IDS solutions. Therefore, privacy aspects in using a cloud-based IDS are minimized compared to solutions that redirect the whole traffic to the cloud.

In the first step each SDN-C will decide autonomously, without including previous IDS results or decisions from earlier SDN-Cs. Later a connection between them will be established to enhance detection capabilities and design the SDN-Cs as a distributed controller.

Use-Cases. Meeting requirements of various deployment scenarios enhances applicability of our proposed architecture and helps to improve the continuous development process. However, we will start implementing a very narrow-focused deployment and enhance it based on our findings and additional use-cases.

– **Software as a Service (SaaS)** products like web-hosting, e-mail or financial management provider are usually accessible from all over the world. In addition, these services seem to be easily configurable, also by people not familiar with security principles.

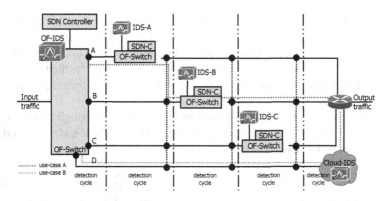

Fig. 1. Architecture Overview including Example Paths

- **Platform as a Service (PaaS)** providers in most cases access to a pre-configured machine regardless of the underlying infrastructure (virtual/ physical). Users of PaaS require a rare understanding of configuring these systems and knowledge in securing them, but gain significant freedom in choosing applications running on top.
- **Company's Internet Access (CIA)** Companies providing services to customers and make Internet access available to employees are responsible for (amongst others) securing their network against attacks or attackers trying to gather customer data. Furthermore, they have to satisfy their customers by meeting SLAs as contracted (e.g., availability, response time).

Service Chaining. Composing a sequence of successive security functions raises immediately concerns about (a) trustworthiness of each security function and (b) the right and entire processing of a composed chain. Therefore, our approach will utilize the benefits of SDN and distributed controllers to establish a verifiable chain of security functions. RQ5 is the core of this aspect and enables adaptability.

4   Concluding Remarks and Perspectives

Since the importance of security raises if more and more companies push their data and processing capabilities into cloud services, our approach tries to provide a solution to inspect traffic by various IDSs including cloud-based IDSs. Finally, it will redirect or block attack traffic at the first point of occurrence in the monitored network. Our proposed solution is also relevant since DDoS attacks are getting more and more popular.

As a next step, we need to investigate statistics derived from OpenFlow in order to detect attacks. At this point a trade-off between detection rate and performance of the OpenFlow device is essential to provide an effective solution. Furthermore, a mechanism needs to be investigated that decides about the next

IDS in the detection process, to be adaptive. Later an evaluation needs to be done regarding the involvement of cloud-based IDSs. Therefore, we will investigate mechanisms to prove cloud-based IDSs performance and reliability. An interesting part of research is the verification of the path the traffic took. In that context, an investigation of service chaining and verification techniques needs to take place.

We envision, as extension of the work in this PhD, a thorough study of SLA restrictions and verification of legal requirements in introducing cloud-based IDS solutions needs to be investigated.

Acknowledgment. This work was partly funded by FLAMINGO, a Network of Excellence project (ICT-318488) supported by the European Commission under its Seventh Framework Programme.

References

1. Akamai - Q4 2014 State of the Internet Security Report,
   http://www.stateoftheinternet.com/resources-web-security-2014-q4-internet-security-report.html (last accessed on January 28, 2015)
2. Arbor Networks - Worldwide Infrastructure Security Report (2014),
   http://pages.arbornetworks.com/rs/arbor/images/WISR2014.pdf
3. Bro Network Security Monitor, http://www.bro.org/ (last accessed on January 28, 2015)
4. Cloudflare, Inc., https://www.cloudflare.com/ (last accessed on January 28, 2015)
5. Franklin Morris, Infographic: SMB Cloud Adoption Trends in (2014),
   http://www.pcworld.com/article/2685792/infographic-smb-cloud-adoption-trends-in-2014.html (last accessed on January 28, 2015)
6. Snort, https://www.snort.org/ (last accessed on January, 28 2015)
7. Suricata IDS/IPS, http://www.suricata-ids.org/ (last accessed on January 28, 2015)
8. AbuHmed, T., Mohaisen, A., Nyang, D.: A survey on deep packet inspection for intrusion detection systems. arXiv preprint arXiv:0803.0037 (2008)
9. Braga, R., Mota, E., Passito, A.: Lightweight DDoS flooding attack detection using NOX/OpenFlow. In: 2010 IEEE 35th Conference on Local Computer Networks (LCN), pp. 408–415. IEEE (2010)
10. Feamster, N.: Outsourcing home network security. In: Proceedings of the 2010 ACM SIGCOMM Workshop on Home Networks, pp. 37–42. ACM (2010)
11. François, J., Dolberg, L., Festor, O., Engel, T.: Network Security through Software Defined Networking: a Survey. In: IIT Real-Time Communications (RTC) Conference-Principles, Systems and Applications of IP Telecommunications (IPT-Comm). ACM
12. Fry, C., Nystrom, M.: Security Monitoring. O'Reilly Media, Inc. (2009)
13. Giotis, K., Argyropoulos, C., Androulidakis, G., Kalogeras, D., Maglaris, V.: Combining OpenFlow and sFlow for an effective and scalable anomaly detection and mitigation mechanism on SDN environments. Computer Networks 62, 122–136 (2014)
14. Kreutz, D., Ramos, F., Verissimo, P.: Towards secure and dependable software-defined networks. In: Proceedings of the Second ACM SIGCOMM Workshop on Hot Topics in software Defined Networking, pp. 55–60. ACM (2013)

15. Schehlmann, L., Baier, H.: COFFEE: A Concept based on OpenFlow to Filter and Erase Events of botnet activity at high-speed nodes. In: GI-Jahrestagung, pp. 2225–2239 (2013)
16. Scott-Hayward, S., O'Callaghan, G., Sezer, S.: SDN security: A survey. In: 2013 IEEE SDN for Future Networks and Services (SDN4FNS), pp. 1–7. IEEE (2013)
17. Sperotto, A., Schaffrath, G., Sadre, R., Morariu, C., Pras, A., Stiller, B.: An Overview of IP Flow-Based Intrusion Detection. IEEE Communications Surveys Tutorials 12(3), 343–356 (2010)

Towards a Cyber-Physical Resilience Framework
for Smart Grids

Ivo Friedberg[1,2(✉)], Kieran McLaughlin[1], and Paul Smith[2]

[1] Queen's University Belfast, Belfast, UK
{ifriedberg01,kieran.mclaughlin}@qub.ac.uk
[2] AIT Austrian Institute of Technology, Vienna, Austria
firstname.lastname@ait.ac.at

Abstract. As modern power grids move towards becoming a *smart grid*, there is an increasing reliance on the data that is transmitted and processed by ICT systems. This reliance introduces new digital attack vectors. Many of the proposed approaches that aim to address this problem largely focus on applying well-known ICT security solutions. However, what is needed are approaches that meet the complex concerns of the smart grid as a *cyber-physical system*. Furthermore, to support the automatic control loops that exist in a power grid, similarly automatic security and resilience mechanisms are needed that rely on minimal operator intervention. The research proposed in this paper aims to develop a framework that ensures resilient smart grid operation in light of successful cyber-attacks.

1 Introduction

Power systems are one of the most critical infrastructures in our society. Priority lies on the stable operation of any power system, ensuring *(i)* human safety, *(ii)* availability and *(iii)* equipment safety [10]. With the shift towards distributed, renewable energy sources, extensive use is made of information and communication technology (ICT) infrastructures to enable enhanced control strategies and energy services. Embedded systems that once worked independently now form an interconnected and interdependent part of the *smart grid*. However, systems such as smart grids, where ICT components control the operation of physical entities so called cyber-physical systems are increasingly being targeted by sophisticated cyber-attacks [4]. Thus, to provide resilience – the ability to maintain acceptable operation in the face of faults and challenges [5] – during successful cyber-attacks on smart grids is an operationally critical problem.

This cyber-physical nature of the smart grid introduces a range of new challenges to ensure grid stability in light of cyber-attacks. One especially hard problem lies in managing both the physical (power) system and the cyber system, in order to provide a comprehensive resilience strategy. Without addressing this problem it is not possible to effectively address the risks caused by the interdependency between both systems. However, current research in the area is either focused on ensuring the robustness of control loops for the physical power

© IFIP International Federation for Information Processing 2015
S. Latré et al. (Eds.): AIMS 2015, LNCS 9122, pp. 140–144, 2015.
DOI: 10.1007/978-3-319-20034-7_15

system (e.g., [9]) or securing the ICT systems. Efforts to secure the ICT systems in this domain largely focus on the prevention [8] or detection [12,3] of cyber-attacks – limited attention is paid to what steps should be taken to ensure grid stability when an attack is successful. In ICT systems, this problem is often left to be solved by human operators. The control loops in power grids – e.g., the Automatic Generation Control (AGC) in Energy Management Systems (EMSs) – currently issue control commands on the order of seconds [6]. This makes timely manual intervention by human operators quite difficult, if not impossible.

Ten *et al.* [7] propose an integrated security framework for power grids. The authors highlight operational blocks of the framework, but the interaction between these blocks is not clearly defined. A data model is needed to tailor the framework to a concrete infrastructure. Furthermore, the authors limit the analysis of the monitored data to anomaly detection. This approach is limiting because current power systems and ICT systems have well-known (non-anomaly based) security and detection mechanisms in place. Sridhar and Manimaran propose an automatic attack mitigation approach that addresses attacks on the AGC control loop [6]. While the described attack scenario leverages the cyber-physical design of the system under evaluation, the mitigation approach operates only on measurement data from the physical part of the system. Furthermore, a broader approach is needed to extend resilient operation to different control loops.

In this paper, we propose a novel cyber-physical resilience framework for smart grids. The framework aims to ensure acceptable levels of grid operation, even in the case of successful and targeted cyber-attacks. The novelty of our work lies in the integration of a synergistic approach linking the cyber and physical systems of a smart grid and in particular deriving a method intended for response and mitigation, rather than prevention and detection. In particular the focus lies on response and mitigation, rather than prevention and detection of the negative effects from successful cyber-attacks on physical system components or their control loops.

2   Proposed Research: A Cyber-Physical Resilience Framework

Our cyber-physical resilience framework consists of a *system model* and a *resilience control loop*. The system model has two main parts: *(i)* a *generic* system model that is provided with the framework; and *(ii)* a *specific* system model that has to be derived from the generic model when the framework is applied to a target infrastructure. The purpose of the model is to describe the necessary domain knowledge to realise the framework and to define the data structures that are transferred between the functional blocks that realise the control loop. The development of the generic model will be one major challenge for this research.

The operation of the grid is managed by the resilience control loop, which is depicted in Fig. 1. It interacts with both the ICT and physical systems of a smart grid to detect and mitigate cyber-attacks. Its functionality can be described as follows. Both the physical and ICT systems of the *Grid* will be monitored using

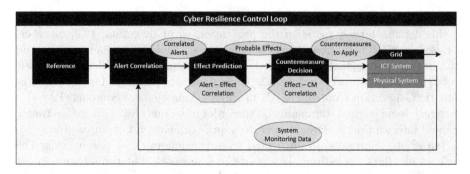

Fig. 1. The control loop at the center of our resilience framework. Rectangular blocks indicate the functional blocks in the loop, while ellipses (transferred data) and hexagons (domain knowledge) mark where parts of the system model will be used.

various systems. For example, for the ICT systems, existing security solutions will be used, such as intrusion detection systems. Meanwhile, for the physical systems various parameters (e.g., voltage, active and reactive power, frequency or phase) will be monitored. Additionally, existing security algorithms in the EMS (e.g., state estimation or bad data detection) [11] can be used to trigger alerts in the case of unexpected behaviour. We foresee one of the major challenges is choosing the right monitoring techniques at the different points of the cyber-physical system. This monitoring needs to be extensive, in order to get a comprehensive view of the whole cyber-physical system, but as limited as possible to make real time correlation feasible.

All *System Monitoring Data* is transferred to the *Alert Correlation* function. Additional information about operational metrics is provided from the *Reference*. The reference data is used to understand the status of the power system based on the collected physical measurements. It contains optimal, acceptable and critical ranges for the various physical measurements as well as operational constraints of the system. In the *Alert Correlation* function, information provided from both parts of the cyber-physical system is analyzed and correlated. The result of this phase is a set of alerts. An alert in this context is a signal that indicates a deviation from optimal system behaviour. The set of possible alerts is defined in the system model. The main challenges associated with realising the *Alert Correlation* function include determining the correct interpretation of physical measurement values during the course of operation, and the timely correlation of monitoring data from the ICT domain and physical domain.

The *Effect Prediction* functionality processes the correlated alerts and predicts the operational behaviour of the grid to detect potentially critical developments, so called effects. An effect is seen as a critical operational state that, if reached, would violate the definition of resilient operation, as defined by the *Reference*. Here we see the major challenge to be the development of an algorithm that estimates the future state of the grid, based on the alerts triggered by the current system state.

Finally, the predicted effects are transmitted to the *Countermeasure Decision* function. Here the available countermeasures are evaluated based on the set of predicted system effects. A decision is taken on which countermeasures to apply. Arguably, for resilient operation it is not required to tackle the root cause of a problem. It can be a valid strategy to do so, but often the root cause cannot be automatically detected or eliminated. Rather, the highest priority of the applied countermeasures (to both the cyber and physical systems) is to mitigate the imminent threat to stable system operation. One challenge will be to identify applicable and effective countermeasures in each domain. Furthermore, applying an automatic countermeasure could result in the non-optimal operation of the grid. Therefore, the decision needs to aim for the least limiting countermeasure that is sufficient to mitigate the effect.

3 Research Methodology

We propose to take a practical approach to evaluating the resilience framework. A test setup, including a power generator and a Phasor Measurement Unit (PMU), will be developed, based on the work of Best *et al.* [2]. The goal will be to detect a set of attacks on a synchronized, but islanded generator. The effects of such attacks can range from outages in the island to equipment damage when the generator is reconnected to the mains supply whilst not synchronized. Countermeasures will be developed to automatically mitigate these risks. To ensure that the lab experiments are representative for attacks in the wild, they will be based on officially published threat scenarios (e.g. the *Electric Sector Failure Scenarios and Impact Analyses* by NESCOR [1]) and performed with modern protocols like IEC 61850. Measuring the effectiveness of the proposed framework will be performed in two ways. Physical (e.g., phase, current or frequency) and operational metrics (e.g. thresholds or set-points) will be used to evaluate the timely effectiveness of the framework in countering the critical effects of successful cyber-attacks. Second, we will develop experimental scenarios that will allow us to compare our framework to related work, such as that discussed earlier.

4 Conclusion

In this paper, we have argued for the need for a cyber-physical resilience framework for smart grids, and presented our initial findings for developing such a framework. The expected impact of this research is an increased resilience of future power systems against cyber-attacks. This resilience is needed to successfully realize the vision of a smart grid. Without it, smart grids will either be realized in a limited way, or the increased use of ICT technology in the power domain will open the means for cyber-attacks with significant societal impact. From a scientific point of view, this research aims to make new advances in cyber-physical system resilience. Results of this research could be extended to address emerging threats or applied to other application domains of cyber-physical systems.

Acknowledgments. This research is funded by the EU FP7 SPARKS project.

References

1. Technical Working Group 1. Electric Sector Failure Scenarios and Impact Analyses. Technical report, NESCOR (June 2014)
2. Best, R.J., Morrow, D.J., Laverty, D.M., Crossley, P.A.: Synchrophasor Broadcast Over Internet Protocol for Distributed Generator Synchronization. IEEE Transactions on Power Delivery 25(4), 2835–2841 (2010)
3. Friedberg, I., Skopik, F., Settanni, G., Fiedler, R.: Combating advanced persistent threats: From network event correlation to incident detection. Computers & Security 48, 35–57 (2015)
4. Lee, R., Assante, M., Connway, T.: ICS CP/PE (Cyber-to-Physical or Process Effects) case study paper – German Steel Mill Cyber Attack. Technical report, SANS ICS (December 2014)
5. Smith, P., Hutchison, D., Sterbenz, J.P.G., Scholler, M., Fessi, A., Karaliopoulos, M., Lac, C., Plattner, B.: Network Resilience: A Systematic Approach. IEEE Communications Magazine 49(7), 88–97 (2011)
6. Sridhar, S., Govindarasu, M.: Model-Based Attack Detection and Mitigation for Automatic Generation Control. IEEE Transactions on Smart Grid 5(2), 580–591 (2014)
7. Ten, C.-W., Manimaran, G., Liu, C.-C.: Cybersecurity for Critical Infrastructures: Attack and Defense Modeling. IEEE Transactions on Systems, Man and Cybernetics, Part A: Systems and Humans 40(4), 853–865 (2010)
8. Vukovic, O., Sou, K.C., Dan, G., Sandberg, H.: Network-layer Protection Schemes Against Stealth Attacks on State Estimators in Power Systems. In: 2011 IEEE International Conference on Smart Grid Communications (SmartGridComm), pp. 184–189 (October 2011)
9. Wang, D., Guan, X., Liu, T., Gu, Y., Shen, C., Xu, Z.: Extended Distributed State Estimation: A Detection Method Against Tolerable False Data Injection Attacks in Smart Grids. Energies 7, 1517–1538 (2014)
10. Wei, D., Lu, Y., Jafari, M., Skare, P., Rohde, K.: An Integrated Security System of Protecting Smart Grid Against Cyber Attacks. In: Innovative Smart Grid Technologies (ISGT 2010), pp. 1–7 (January 2010)
11. Wood, A.J., Wollenberg, B.F.: Power Generation, Operation, and Control, 3rd edn. John Wiley & Sons (2012)
12. Zhu, B., Sastry, S.: SCADA-specific Intrusion Detection/Prevention Systems: A Survey and Taxonomy. In: Proceedings of the 1st Workshop on Secure Control Systems, (SCS) (2010)

Characterizing the IPv6 Security Landscape by Large-Scale Measurements

Luuk Hendriks[✉], Anna Sperotto, and Aiko Pras

Design and Analysis of Communication Systems (DACS),
University of Twente, Enschede, The Netherlands
{luuk.hendriks,a.sperotto,a.pras}@utwente.nl

Abstract. Networks are transitioning from IP version 4 to the new version 6. Fundamental differences in the protocols introduce new security challenges with varying levels of evidence. As enabling IPv6 in an existing network is often already challenging on the functional level, security aspects are overlooked, even those that are emphasized in literature. Reusing existing security solutions for IPv4 might seem easy and cost-effective, but is based on the unproven assumption that IPv6 attack traffic features the same characteristics. By performing network measurements and analyzing IPv6 attacks on the network-level, we determine the current state of security in the IPv6 domain. With the inevitable switch to the new protocol version, assessing the applicability of existing security approaches and determining the requirements for new solutions becomes a necessity.

1 Introduction

In this paper we aim to describe our plans on researching the status of IPv6 security by performing measurements. After introducing the subject and the motivation for the work, the goal and research questions are stated and explained in Section 2. The approaches planned in order to answer the questions are explained in Section 3, followed by brief final considerations in Section 4.

The new version 6 of the Internet Protocol (IPv6) is gradually being adopted by the Internet. The successor of the currently most-used IP version 4 (IPv4) is often seen as an expansion in terms of address space, but that is just a one of many changes. Once designed with security in mind, after 20 years of developments and implementations, some question whether IPv6 is indeed more secure than its predecessor. As IPv6 is gaining traction, the amount of malicious traffic transferred over it increases [12]. Besides attacks that are based on aspects of the new protocol, we can expect traditional attacks from IPv4 occurring over IPv6 as well, as many types of these threats abuse features or phenomena on higher layers (e.g., the transport or application layer). In addition to that, the technologies designed to aid in the transitional phase from IPv4 to IPv6 (e.g., tunneling techniques *6to4* and *TEREDO*, among others) come with their own issues [3,6]. Circumvention of firewalls [5] in certain scenarios is a severe example of this. Lastly, another likely source of security issues are end-users not aware

© IFIP International Federation for Information Processing 2015
S. Latré et al. (Eds.): AIMS 2015, LNCS 9122, pp. 145–149, 2015.
DOI: 10.1007/978-3-319-20034-7_16

of IPv6 connectivity on their systems and network [10], making them prone to attacks via unexpected ways.

The new version of the IP protocol itself, as well as its supporting protocols (e.g., the Neighbour Discovery Protocol), have been subjected to research and insecurities have been pointed out in the literature [1,2,6]. These works have described issues and weaknesses, but did not focus on actual occurrences of attempts to exploit them in the Internet. Some research has been done in that area, mainly by measuring so-called *darknets*. A darknet is address space that contains no actual services, but is advertised and routed. Any traffic arriving in such a space can be considered malicious [4]. Although a darknet simplifies the classification of traffic as being either benign or malicious, the fact it contains no actual services is likely to lower the interest of those with bad intents. These studies [4,9,12] do however show an increase in the amount of observed traffic throughout the years.

With this work we intend to research the actual state of security in the IPv6 Internet, and how it can be improved. Besides the shown increase of malicious traffic, our study is also motivated by the imbalance between availability of tools (e.g., the THC hacker toolkit [8] for IPv6, first released in 2005) and countermeasures for weaknesses these tools exploit: the first RFC describing RA-Guard [11] on how to mitigate Router Advertisement-based attacks is dated 2011, and the first version of a BCP concerning rogue DHCPv6 servers [7] was presented in 2012. A comprehensive study of Ullrich et al. [14] divides the known IPv6 problems in 36 security vulnerabilities and 14 privacy issues. With that, 44 possible countermeasures are listed. The large number of countermeasures shows that most issues are technically surmountable, but the possibility of configuration errors or omissions is significant. Furthermore they point out that several concepts within the IPv6 domain are being deprecated now or in the foreseeable future, while many implementations are already running in production. Updates to those implementations are not a given, so even with deprecation of security-impairing aspects in mind, there is no guarantee on how fast the improvements will actually be functional. This further emphasizes the need for real-world measurement-based studies to complement theoretical conclusions.

2   Goal and Research Questions

The goal of the research is **to characterize the IPv6 landscape from a security perspective**, as motivated in the previous section.

The following research questions will be answered:

1. *What types of attacks can be observed over IPv6 on the network-level, and how do they relate to attacks over IPv4?*
2. *Which fraction of the Internet is susceptibility to IPv6-based attacks?*
3. *How can detection of IPv6-based threats be performed?*

The answer to the first research question will give an overview of attacks that are occurring in the Internet, and the attacks that are possible based on attack tools openly available. The gained knowledge is used in the approach to answer question 2. By answering question 2, the level of security in the IPv6 Internet is determined, and the likelihood and severeness of the attacks found in question 1 are assessed. Lastly, by answering question 3, ways of detecting threats in the IPv6 domain are researched, in order to improve the overall level of security of the IPv6 Internet.

3 Approach

Our approach is mainly based on performing measurements. Answering the first question will comprise of two separate, simultaneous forms of measurements. By doing large-scale passive measurements, attacks over IPv6 are observed. The vast address space reduces the probability of malicious traffic entering the monitored networks. By focussing on address space that has been allocated for several years (e.g., the SURFnet network) the chances of obtaining useful data increase. To further increase possibilities of acquiring data, a reactive system might be used, i.e., a system acting on incoming IPv6 traffic regardless of the destination. A similar approach in [12], based on dynamic instantiation in honeynets, showed promising results. Traffic will be collected in forms of both packet captures and flow records, increasing the flexibility in the analysis. As this process involves a certain waiting time, and the possibility of not resulting in sufficient data to analyze, lab experiments will be conducted parallel to the passive measurements. By collecting and analyzing attack tools openly available, signatures can be created to aid in both the analysis of the data obtained via the passive measurements, as well as answering research questions 2 and 3.

The goal of question 2 is to determine to what extend the observed attacks can be effective in reality, or, how well protected the Internet is from them. The question is answered by performing active measurements, where the exact form of measurements is determined by the outcome of the first research question. If a large amount of attacks is observed via the passive measurements, these attacks will be characterized. If on the other hand the results from the passive measurements are not substantial, characteristics from the collected and analyzed attack tools are used. By smartly [14] scanning parts of the IPv6 address space, systems connected via IPv6 are found. The share of vulnerable hosts is determined based on the attacks' characteristics. For example, we might find attacks based on abusing services on the application layer. Operators might use specific addressing schemes within their network, where part of the address represents the service running on that system [13]. Examples are DNS services being deployed on 2001:db8::100:53, or HTTP on 2001:db8::100:80, thus the last field representing the transport layer port. Performing smart scans possibly provides insights in this scenario. In the case that attacks are tailored towards exploiting vulnerabilities in implementations of IPv6 network stacks, vulnerability is related to (the version of) the operation system on possible target hosts. Fingerprinting of operating systems will result in more useful information to determine the share of hosts possibly subjected to this kind of attacks.

The third question finally, assesses the possibilities of detecting the attacks. In this study, the applicability of approaches and solutions from the IPv4 domain is researched. The goal of this question is to research whether new detection technologies are required to ensure security within the IPv6-adopting Internet. For attacks newly introduced with IPv6, we intend to design adequate detection algorithms. The form of input for these algorithms depends on the form of the attacks. If flow-level data is insufficient to perform accurate detection, e.g. because specific headers or payload are key in detecting the attack, packet-level input will be used. The algorithms will be tested by means of implementing a prototype, to be validated with a ground truth. The ground truth again depends on the form of the attack: if attacks have an analogue in the IPv4 domain, existing detection algorithms and tools can provide the ground truth. Otherwise, analysis of logfiles on attacked or compromised end-hosts will provide insights to validate the results of detection on the network-level. If validity is proven, the algorithms might be tested for scalability and performance in larger set-ups, e.g., by deployment on National Research and Educational Network (NREN) links, or at Computer Security Incident Response Teams (CSIRTs).

4   Final Considerations

Within our research, measurements will be conducted in various forms. Performing active measurements will likely raise ethical or perhaps legal questions. Extra consideration or adjustment of plans might be needed if these questions create legitimate limitations. The main research goal as described is to be achieved within the duration of four years, as parts of Ph.D. research. The research is partly funded by the European FLAMINGO[1] project (ICT-FP7 318488) and SURFnet[2].

References

1. Beck, F., Cholez, T., Festor, O., Chrisment, I.: Monitoring the neighbor discovery protocol. In: The Second International Workshop on IPv6 Today-Technology and Deployment-IPv6TD 2007 (2007)
2. Caicedo, C.E., Joshi, J.B., Tuladhar, S.R.: IPv6 security challenges. Computer (2), 36–42 (2009)
3. Elich, M., Velan, P., Jirsik, T., Celeda, P.: An investigation into teredo and 6to4 transition mechanisms: Traffic analysis. In: 2013 IEEE 38th Conference on Local Computer Networks Workshops (LCN Workshops), pp. 1018–1024 (October 2013 2013)
4. Ford, M., Stevens, J., Ronan, J.: Initial Results from an IPv6 Darknet. In: International Conference on Internet Surveillance and Protection, ICISP 2006, pp. 13–17 (2006)
5. Giobbi, R.: Bypassing Firewalls with IPv6 Tunnels (2009), http://www.cert.org/blogs/certcc/post.cfm?EntryID=37 (accessed March 2015)

---

[1] http://www.fp7-flamingo.eu/
[2] http://surfnet.nl

6. Gont, F.: Security implications of IPv6 on IPv4 networks, RFC 7123, Internet Engineering Task Force (2014)
7. Gont, F., et al.: DHCPv6-Shield: Protecting Against Rogue DHCPv6 Servers (2012)
8. Heuse, M.: THC IPv6 attack tool kit, https://www.thc.org/thc-ipv6/ (accessed March 2015)
9. Huston, G.: Background Radiation in IPv6. The ISP Column, APNIC (2010)
10. Krishnan, S., Hoagland, J., Thaler, D.: Security Concerns with IP Tunneling, RFC 6169, Internet Engineering Task Force (2011)
11. Levy-Abegnoli, E., Van de Velde, G., Popoviciu, C., Mohacsi, J.: IPv6 Router Advertisement Guard. Tech. rep., RFC 6105, Internet Engineering Task Force (2011)
12. Schindler, S., Schnor, B., Kiertscher, S., Scheffler, T., Zack, E.: IPv6 network attack detection with HoneydV6. In: Obaidat, M.S., Filipe, J. (eds.) ICETE 2013. CCIS, vol. 456, pp. 252–269. Springer, Heidelberg (2014)
13. SURFnet: Preparing an IPv6 addressing plan (2013), https://www.surf.nl/en/knowledge-and-innovation/knowledge-base/2013/white-paper-preparing-an-ipv6-address-plan.html (accessed March 2015)
14. Ullrich, J., Krombholz, K., Hobel, H., Dabrowski, A., Weippl, E.: IPv6 security: attacks and countermeasures in a nutshell. In: Proceedings of the 8th USENIX Conference on Offensive Technologies, pp. 5–16. USENIX Association (2014)

Author Index